I0805029

CHRONICLES OF COLCHESTER

Chronicles of
Colchester

Inge Schaefer

The History Press

Colchester & Malletts Bay

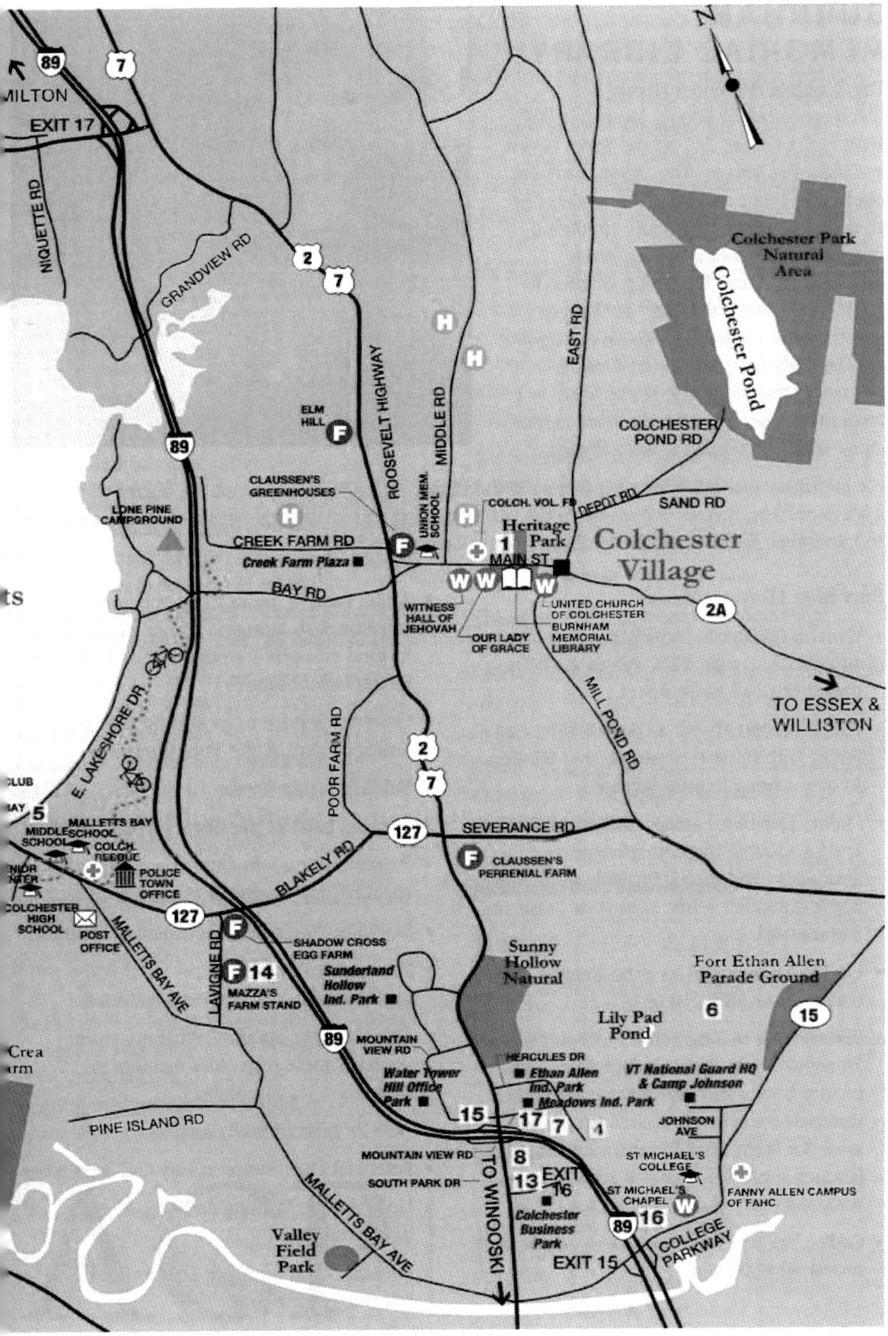
N
89
7
MILTON
EXIT 17
NIQUETTE RD
GRANDVIEW RD
2
7
ROOSEVELT HIGHWAY
MIDDLE RD
EAST RD
Colchester Park Natural Area
Colchester Pond
COLCHESTER POND RD
ELM HILL
CLAUSSEN'S GREENHOUSES
UNION MEM. SCHOOL
COLCH. VOL. FD
DEPOT RD
SAND RD
LONE PINE CAMPGROUND
CREEK FARM RD
Creek Farm Plaza
Heritage Park
1
MAIN ST
Colchester Village
BAY RD
WITNESS HALL OF JEHOVAH
OUR LADY OF GRACE
UNITED CHURCH OF COLCHESTER
BURNHAM MEMORIAL LIBRARY
2A
TO ESSEX & WILLISTON
E. LAKESHORE DR
POOR FARM RD
MILL POND RD
5
MALLETTS BAY SCHOOL
MIDDLE SCHOOL
COLCH. RESCUE
POLICE TOWN OFFICE
COLCHESTER HIGH SCHOOL
POST OFFICE
127
SEVERANCE RD
BLAKELY RD
CLAUSSEN'S PERRENIAL FARM
MALLETTS BAY AVE
LAVIGNE RD
SHADOW CROSS EGG FARM
14
MAZZA'S FARM STAND
Sunderland Hollow Ind. Park
Sunny Hollow Natural
Fort Ethan Allen Parade Ground
6
15
Lily Pad Pond
MOUNTAIN VIEW RD
HERCULES DR
Ethan Allen Ind. Park
VT National Guard HQ & Camp Johnson
Water Tower Hill Office Park
Meadows Ind. Park
17
4
JOHNSON AVE
PINE ISLAND RD
MOUNTAIN VIEW RD
8
ST MICHAEL'S COLLEGE
SOUTH PARK DR
13
EXIT 16
ST MICHAEL'S CHAPEL
FANNY ALLEN CAMPUS OF FAHC
Colchester Business Park
16
COLLEGE PARKWAY
TO WINOOSKI
Valley Field Park
EXIT 15

Published by The History Press
Charleston, SC 29403
www.historypress.net

First published 2009

Back cover image, bottom: Anna White in the early 1900s, standing on a natural stone dock at Goodsell Point. She would wave a lantern to guide her husband Ray on his passenger boat the *Frances Ann. Courtesy of Alta White and Joyce Sweeney.*

Manufactured in the United States

ISBN 978.1.59629.622.0

Library of Congress Cataloging-in-Publication Data

Schaefer, Inge.
Chronicles of Colchester / Inge Schaefer.
p. cm.
ISBN 978-1-59629-622-0
1. Colchester (Vt. : Town)--History. 2. Colchester (Vt. : Town)--Social life and customs. 3. Colchester (Vt. : Town)--Biography. I. Title.
F59.C65S327 2009
974.3'17--dc22
2009041650

CONTENTS

PREFACE

Of the 237 towns in Vermont, Colchester is clearly the largest (there are also nine cities in the state). Colchester is further distinguished by its 27 miles of shoreline on Lake Champlain, the longest shoreline of any community situated on this large, albeit not great, lake. Lake Champlain extends 118 miles from Canada to New York. Ira Allen, brother to Ethan and one of the founders of Vermont and the University of Vermont, was Colchester's first town clerk. These distinctions, along with other notable attributes—such as its many landmarks and early families, whose descendants still walk its streets—are discussed in this book.

Colchester, Vermont, was chartered in 1763, or 246 years ago (this being 2009). The land, however, was first visited by a European 400 years ago, when Samuel de Champlain paddled a canoe into Lake Champlain. In an article written for the *Britannica Online Encyclopedia*, James P. Millard writes that the

> *French explorer, acknowledged founder of the city of Quebec (1608) and consolidator of the French colonies of the New World discovered the lake that bears his name (1609) and made other explorations of what is now northern New York, the Ottawa River and the eastern great lakes.*

Interestingly, Henry Hudson explored what was to become the Hudson River in New York in the same year. It is rousing, to say the least, in this quadricentennial year of Samuel de Champlain's first sighting of Lake Champlain to take a fresh look at Colchester.

Twenty-seven miles of shoreline on Lake Champlain have, over the years, shaped the town's social and financial fortunes. Along these twenty-seven miles lie some of the most breathtaking views of New York's Adirondack Mountains and Vermont's Green Mountains. Commercial shipping of timber, marble and the like has given way over the years to recreational fishing and boating, but the use of the waters of Malletts Bay and the broad lake that surrounds Colchester have only grown in popularity. To help the reader understand the cultural, as well as economic, changes that have taken place since 1763, this book includes a look at both the people and what they built. The reader will find several chapters on the early settling families of Colchester. In each case, descendants of these families still reside on the land of their forefathers, and to this transplanted resident, that fact is amazing. It is with gratitude that I thank these folks—not only for their help with the book or their particular family histories, but also for staying here. They add character and depth to the town and remind us all of its many attributes, not the least of which is its history.

The articles contained herein were originally printed in the *Colchester Chronicle*, the town's first newspaper, which I started in 1985, and in the *Colchester News Magazine*, which I published in the late 1990s. Most of the historical articles were printed in 1996 and 1997, so when possible, the articles have been updated to the current year 2009. The resource information for each is referenced within the article. The following Colchesterites—with patience and kindness—have been willing to answer my questions and set me straight on people, places and things: Becky Munson; Joyce Sweeney; David Coates; Murray Thompson, his wife, Julie Smith, and his dad, Roland Thompson; Ruth Morgan; Sister Irene Dushesneau; Don Fuller; Corky Magoon and the Colchester Historical Society; and staff members of the town, particularly those in the Town Clerk's Office. Others—like Buff Lindau and Liz Scott of St. Michael's College and John Gant, who fell in love with Fort Ethan Allen while living there—came to my rescue as well, so I extend my heartfelt thanks and appreciation to them. Special thanks go to Pat Brace Reed and Hank Schaefer for reviewing the entire text for readability and accuracy. Hank also assisted when it was time to prepare the photos for publishing—a task that always befuddles me.

Newspaper writers in the 1950s described Colchester as a "quiet, rural hamlet." It was, at that time, the twentieth most populous town in the state. In 2009, with more than seventeen thousand residents, it is the second most populous single community in the state after the city of Burlington (Essex and Essex Junction together show a higher number of residents, but that union, as of 2009, had not yet been consummated). Colchester also has the following noteworthy credentials: it is the location of more electronic media stations (radio and television) than any other community in the state; it is home to a hospital, the Fanny Allen campus of the Fletcher Allen Health Center and the nationally renowned St. Michael's College, as well as the recently opened Albany College of Pharmacy; and it is home to the nationally recognized Colchester Bog. It is also the headquarters of the Vermont Army National Guard at Camp Johnson. Despite that, Colchester, to many Vermont citizens, remains a "quiet, rural hamlet," although it is my belief that the Colchester of today more closely resembles Vermont's "sleeping giant."

The articles, therefore, in *Chronicles of Colchester* are intended to present a broad view of a community that will soon celebrate its 250th anniversary (2013). Their diversity is intentional in order to demonstrate the richness of Colchester's history and to imagine its prospects for the future. How will the "giant" awaken? Might it be content to remain "sleeping," thus continuing to lure its citizens and many visitors into believing it to be a "quiet, rural hamlet"? Read on, and then spend time in Colchester, and decide for yourself.

FAMILIES THAT ENDURE

With a population in 2009 of more than seventeen thousand residents, Colchester has witnessed thousands of families passing through its borders. None of those listed as grantees in the town of Colchester on June 7, 1763, by His Excellency Benning Wentworth, governor and commander in chief of the province of New Hampshire in New England acting on behalf of King George III of England, have a presence in Colchester today. Most were considered speculators who sold their land shortly after the charter was signed. Stipulations of the charter as it pertained to the land included that the grantees must "plant and cultivate five Acres of Land with the Term of five Years for every fifty Acres contained in his or their share or Proportion of Land in said Township." "Any white or other Pine Trees" had to be given to the Royal Navy for use in the building of masts. The payment of one shilling for every hundred acres owned was also decreed, as was one ear of corn to be paid on December 25 for each of ten years. Ten of the original grantees had the name Burling, with several named Latham, Lawrence and Bogert. Land for use by two churches was also set aside in the charter, along with five hundred acres for Wentworth himself.

While none of those families helped develop the town, Remember Baker, cousin to Ira and Ethan Allen, did, and it is rumored that one of his descendants was a resident of the town until the late 1900s. Ira's wife and children moved to Irasburg, Vermont, after he left the state for Pennsylvania. Ethan's family stayed, and he was buried in 1789 in Burlington. No history of Colchester would be complete without at least a mention of the infamous

Captain Stephen Mallett, after whom Malletts Bay and much of the area surrounding it, is named. In a 1955 article, Joseph A. Citro wrote:

> *according to legend, Mallett, like* [Captain] *Kidd, was a high-seas swashbuckler who—for some reason—chose to retire in Vermont. He built a home and ran a rough tavern on what is now Malletts Bay.*

He was French, and his name has been spelled Malet, Mallett and, as Citro notes, "occasionally Jean-Pierre Mallet." Vermont historian Ralph Nading Hill suggests that he may have settled in Colchester before the American Revolution. Hill writes:

> *Captain Mallett was apparently a man of considerable independence of spirit; he feared no one and acknowledged allegiance neither to the English King nor to the American Colonies. It seems that he never accepted the Treaty of Peace which gave control over his lands to the English; his sympathies were on the side of rebellion, for he welcomed spies and smugglers into his home all through the Revolutionary period.*

A pirate, scoundrel, or just a grouchy hermit—the truth about the man after whom so much in Colchester is named remains a mystery.

Other early settlers, however, whose names have long been associated with the town, include Munson, Severance, Wolcott (or Woolcot), Austin, Hine, Law, Stanton, Brownell, Thompson, Porter and Coates. Little is known about some of them, but for those whose relatives still live here, the following look at life in Colchester since the early 1800s is offered.

THE MUNSON FAMILY

Everything Was Different Then

"I'm the fifth generation Munson living in Colchester and I'm the last," said Walter Munson in an interview in February 1997. His prophesy was fulfilled on December 19, 2000, when he passed away at the age of ninety-eight years. With no other living descendants of the William Munson family still residing in town, and with no children of his own,

Walter smiled on that February day in '97 and said, "You're looking at the end of the line."

Fortunately, his wife, Becky Munson, is a genealogy buff and has kept a careful record of her husband's family and other settling families of the area. Not to be outdone, Walter wrote a book on his hunting and fishing recollections and was a founding member of the town's historical society. The very house that Becky and Walter shared for many years is, itself, of historical significance. "I do believe the kitchen was originally a log cabin with the brick portion coming later (1823) because the floor's wood planks are this wide," Walter said, as he gestured with arms to describe a three-foot-wide plank. Becky has since confirmed the log cabin aspect of the house.

A recently renovated barn on the property was constructed long before 1850. The commonly called "Munson Cemetery," located up the hill from the homestead, is described in Ruth Wright's book *Colchester, Vermont: Ice-Cap to Interstate* as follows:

> *In 1804 the Selectmen of Colchester laid out a burying ground, for a long time known as Maple View Cemetery, 40 rods south of Munson's Mill on the top of a hill...containing 1 acre and 9 rods of ground.*

"Most of the family is buried up there," said Walter, including his first wife of twenty-seven years, Alice Munson.

According to a 1938 *Burlington Free Press* article, William Munson came to Colchester as early as 1790 from Dover, New Hampshire, with twelve cents in his pocket and an axe over his back. According to Becky, however, William Munson came to Colchester in 1791 from Portsmouth, Maine, and lived by the Winooski Falls part of town. (Winooski Falls was part of Colchester until 1922.) There, he met his wife, Ama Brownell (called Amy). There is agreement that William first worked for Ira Allen in his sawmill and that he was soon working for himself clearing land and building mills. Two of his brothers—Theodore (who later moved to Illinois with several other Munsons) and Daniel—also came to Vermont, along with their sister, Mary, who never married. There were fourteen children from the William and Ama Munson union; the firstborn son was named William (as was to become a tradition). William Brownell Munson married Anjulina Day, daughter of Alfred Day, who lived in the same general area of the Falls. Their firstborn, William Day Munson, married Julia Henderson, who was rumored to be a descendant of Caleb Henderson, a spy for the British and a Loyalist. William and Anjulina had five children total; two

Colonel William D. Munson (1833–1903) served in the Civil War and, later, as Colchester's town clerk. *Courtesy of Rebecca Munson.*

babies died in infancy and were buried in the family cemetery. One child died in the infamous Andersonville, Georgia prisoner of war camp during the Civil War.

William Day Munson's first son, William Henry, was Walter's father. There was also a daughter, Ella, who died at one year old, and Minnie May, who married Charles Wright and lived on Main Street. William Henry married Mertie Belle Thompson, daughter of a miller (the mill on Mill Pond Road, formerly called Old Country Road). Their first son was again called William, using as a middle name Herbert after grandfather Herbert Thompson (of the Middle Road Thompsons). Sisters Mildred May and Marian and brother Walter Cobb completed the family.

In Wright's book, settler William Munson is first mentioned in reference to being appointed to a committee to settle some land disputes, and together with Francis Childs, Simeon Hine, Elnathan Keys and Eli Baker, the committee reported that Ira Allen, "who pretends to be the former clerk of the Proprietors, refused to give any satisfaction or deliver any papers relative to said interest, if any he had." This same committee later presented a "Plan of the Town and a 'Field Book' accompanying the same, from a survey made under their inspection," which was approved. Munson

William and Mertie Munson leave their homestead (which remains today on Munson Road near the village) and head for Burlington, circa late 1800s. *Courtesy of Rebecca Munson.*

was also to serve as constable of the town, as town clerk and as the town's representative to the legislature in 1806.

A white farmhouse located on what was then called Old Stage Road, now Roosevelt Highway, Route 2A, is on the original 165 acres of land that Munson owned. He left the land to his son Wallace, who deeded it to his brother John, who in turn, in 1841, built the house currently owned by Carol and Clint Reichard. John sold it to his sister Clara and her husband, Lemuel Platt. The land across the road from the house is called Munson Flats. William built his house farther down the road across from the Champlain Farms store on the Route 7 side. According to Becky, William Munson, the first Munson to live in Colchester, died in 1831.

In 1833, William Brownell Munson served on the Colchester Select Board and the school board when the total number of students was 475, including those students from the Winooski area. He was a surveyor and also operated the sawmill on Indian Brook at the intersection of the County Road (Route 2A) and West Road (now Lakeshore Drive) across from Walter's house.

William Day Munson died in 1903 before grandson Walter could get to know him. A graduate of Norwich University in Vermont, army captain

William D. commanded a volunteer company called the "Colchester Light Artillery," according to Wright's book. In 1996, Becky, while rummaging through the barn, discovered the official document acknowledging the company and listing all of its members. In 1863, William D. was promoted to lieutenant colonel and fought and was wounded in the Battle of Gettysburg, after which his Thirteenth Regiment was mustered out of military service. "Youths of Company D, returning to Colchester, received a popular heroes' welcome and were served a bountiful supper in the basement of the Winooski church," Wright noted.

Walter also knows that his grandfather was a musician (violinist) traveling with his son down South to play in opera houses in Georgia and North Carolina. Walter's father, William Henry, returned home first. He suggested by letter to his father, who was still on the road, that they purchase the home—long since occupied by Walt and Becky—from Phelps for the asking price of $3,000. Walter recalled that everyone in Colchester in those days was related somehow: "You had to marry whoever was in town because it was hard to get anywhere else." Grandfather Munson was the Congregational church choir director with his daughter, Minnie, at the organ. He also directed the Colchester band. Concerts were given on the bandstand located between the Baptist and Congregational churches on Main Street. The bandstand has since been moved to the former parade grounds at Fort Ethan Allen.

According to Wright's book:

> *Dances were held at Colonel Munson's and at the Town Hall…the dances did not get into full swing until about 10 o'clock and often continued until 4 a.m.…Col. Munson and the singer…were considered very handsome dancers.*

Walter attributed his love of dancing, hunting and fishing to the grandfather he never knew.

In his book, *75 Years of Hunting and Fishing,* Walter wrote:

> *Born in 1902 on the small farm where I still live, with a brook, and in those days a small mill pond behind the barn, it was only natural that I took to fishing as soon as I could cut an alder pole. I would wander down after minnows, bullheads, rock bass, suckers, etc. Of course, it was a constant worry to Mother, but I only fell in once and my sister Marian rescued me.*

Later in the book he mused:

> *Back when Fort Ethan Allen was an active cavalry post, some of the officers owned foxhounds which frequently ran foxes on the hills south of the farm, oftentimes in the evening. I loved to sit outside and listen to them. Guess I inherited it from Grandfather Munson who was an avid foxhunter.*

With a twinkle in his eye, Walter said he also "lived for the summers so I could pay just a $1.00 for a whole evening at the Bayside Pavilion listening and dancing to the big bands and meeting a new girl."

He remembered a time when his older brother, William, and sister Mildred would go off to Burlington High School on a Monday morning with their clothes and food for the week and board with someone in town. By the time he and his sister Marian were ready, Essex Junction High School was open and easier to go to each day by walking a mile to the village, "and then we went with an 'old maid' schoolteacher in her horse and buggy," he recalled. "Later a bunch of us kids would ride our own horses to school and in the winter we used a sled pulled by a team of horses. Inside the shed we had a stand-up heater to keep warm." Smiling, Walter noted:

> *Everything was different then—we knew everybody in town—maybe not everyone in Malletts Bay because we couldn't get there as easily. We'd get ice from the Bay and play ice hockey using a frozen cow plop for a puck. Everyone had farm animals in those days, a few cows, pigs, horses, and chickens.*

His sister, Mildred, would become a teacher, beginning her career at the Blakely School (junction of Blakely and Lavigne Roads) for ten dollars a week. Marian became a music teacher, and brother Bill became a businessman. Walter chose farming. "It [Colchester] has just changed so dramatically in the last one hundred years. It's now a small city," Walter commented in response to a question about his reflections of the town's growth.

In 1986, ten years before the 1997 interview, I asked Walter what he thought of the future of farming in Colchester. A man of few words, Walter said, "There isn't any." Walter was eighty-three years old then. He still had twenty-five cows but added, "When my farmhand goes, so goes the Guernseys."

In 1997, at the time of his last in-depth interview, the Guernseys were gone. Walter was ninety-four years old, quick witted and in good health, and he still attended Colchester Historical Society meetings with Becky. They both worked diligently to keep the memories of an earlier time alive by preserving log books that date back to the first Colchester Munson and reconstructing their and the town's histories through old records, photos and artifacts (Indian heads found on the property) and by racking their collective memories of a time fondly recalled as "the good old days."

The Thompson Family

Two Hundred and Ten Years—but Who's Counting?

The Thompsons are among the town's oldest families residing on one of its oldest farms on Middle Road in the village. According to Roland "Rollie" Thompson, the farm was originally purchased in April 1797 by his great-great-grandfather Thomas Greenough. Greenough was married to Rhoda (Arnold), a woman whose family had come to Rhode Island with Roger Williams.

The original homestead was just southwest of the present house on some slightly higher ground. "It wasn't much of a house, had a bearskin for a front door," says Roland, still spry and alert in 2009 at ninety-two years of age. A more permanent house was built on the present site in the early 1800s. In 1834, Greenough sold the farm to his son, Stephen Greeno. The spelling of the name had changed since 1797. Whether that was the intent of Stephen or a phonetic spelling by the town clerk registering the deed is unknown.

Issac Thompson (Rollie's other great-great-grandfather) came to Colchester from Dover, New Hampshire, circa 1810. Issac married Eunice Parcher, and they had a daughter, Eunice, and a son, Noah. It was Noah (born in 1810) who later married Hannah Greenough (or Greeno), and their son, Murray Eldridge Thompson, was Roland's grandfather. Murray E. fought at the Battle of Gettysburg in July 1863 and returned to Colchester at the end of his enlistment.

The *Gazetteer Business Directory of Chittenden County* for 1882–83, records the following of Issac:

> *He was a soldier in the war of 1812, and was present in the battle of Plattsburgh. He located upon the old Thompson homestead, now owned by*

Lawrence, Roberta, Roland and Noah Thompson, circa 1920s. *Courtesy of Joyce Sweeney.*

> *W.W. Wallace (his son), and built the first house thereon, of plank, during the cold summer of 1816 and with others suffered much in consequence of the scarcity of grain caused by that unfruitful season. He was twice married, and reared a family of fourteen children.*

According to Rollie, Issac settled in the bay area on the village side of Interstate I-89, near Lone Pine Campsites, so it is not clear exactly which homestead this was.

It appears that in 1865 Stephen Greeno sold the farm to William Henderson, a Burlington lawyer, after which the Greeno family moved west. It has been reported that the Thompsons also moved west, but Roland says that this is incorrect. Murray lived here in Colchester and on the family homestead. Roland believes that he may have been working the farm for shares until he had enough money to repurchase the farm. In 1867, the homestead burned down and was rebuilt on the same foundation where the house currently stands. In 1882, Murray purchased the farm; by 1890, he had fully paid for it.

Although there was a break in ownership from 1865 to 1882, the farm has been worked by the Thompson family since 1797, well over two hundred years. Roland has a brother, Noah, who lives nearby in Essex, Vermont. The Colchester Thompsons—Roland, his son, Murray, and daughter-in-law, Julie Smith—continue to farm this land in 2009. When Roland was asked what he thought about his son continuing the family tradition of farming, he responded, "It's the way I expected things to be."

Rollie Thompson in 1997. *Photo by Inge Schaefer.*

Rollie Thompson has become known in Colchester for his philosophical one-liners that are both witty and true. Here's one "Rollieism" that he shared at his ninetieth birthday: "You don't have to know anything to have an opinion." May Roland Thompson, his son, Murray, and now Murray's son, as he grows in the town of his ancestors, continue to share their opinions for many generations to come.

The Severance Family

"A Family that's Been Here for as Long as Most Can Remember"

With the peace that followed the Revolutionary War, new settlers began to once again migrate to upstate Vermont and Colchester. Among them were the brothers Ebenezer and John Severance, arriving in Colchester about 1800 from Hartford, Connecticut. The population—including Winooski Falls, which was then part of Colchester—was about 349 people, according to Ruth Wright.

"Ebenezer came with his wife, Jerusha, and their two children. They had six more born here," recall Malcolm and his sister, Joyce Severance Sweeney, descendants of the early settlers. The children were Jane, Samuel, John, George, Mary, Angeline, Nixen and Joseph. "Our father, John Herbert Severance, born in 1895, was the son of Edwin Severance Jr., who was the son of John Martin Severance Jr. He was the son of John Martin Sr., who was the son of either John or George," says Malcolm.

Malcolm remembers his father telling him about how, as an eleven-year-old, he found his grandfather dead in the field, apparently of a heart attack while getting the cows in the pasture. "His hair was white and his face was so black," Malcom's father told him. His grandmother, Celia, got her son, Percy, who was a pharmacist, to come home and run the farm. Malcolm and Joyce's father worked the farm with Uncle Percy until he married Juanita Bombard, who had grown up on what is now the Eugene Button Farm on Route 7. They then leased the Thompson farm on Middle Road.

When he had built up a bit of a herd—maybe twelve or fifteen Guernsey milking cows—Malcolm's father bought a farm in 1930 on Route 7 and Old Country Road (known today as Roosevelt Highway

Joyce Sweeney helps her dad, John Herbert Severance, cultivate the land, circa 1940s. *Courtesy of Joyce Sweeney.*

and Severance Road). "I can still remember helping to move the piano from the Thompson farm to our new home," says Malcolm. The herd, numbering eighty with over fifty milkers, was sold in 1964. The Severance homestead, the big white house on the southeast corner (it used to be on the northeast corner before Severance Road was relocated), minus the barn that burned down in 1979, was sold with one acre of land in 1982. Forty-nine acres of the farm had been sold in the 1960s to the Gunelics, who started the Sunderland Gardens Nursery.

While there are plenty of Severances throughout the state, Malcolm and Joyce are the only descendants of Ebenezer and John still living in Colchester. "We suspect the road was named 'Severance' for a family that has been here as long as most can remember," says Joyce.

Of life on the farm, Joyce remembers being able to ride her horse in the mid-1940s down Lost Nation, Bay, Depot and Blakely Roads, all of which were dirt roads at the time. "If we wanted to go to Essex Junction, we'd go through the village or through the woods [now Westbury Trailer Park]. We also used to ski on Sunderland Hollow. It was all pasture halfway down the hill."

"I still worked on the farm while I was in college after World War II," says Malcolm.

The Severance kids enjoy the ski slopes of Sunderland Hollow in 1945. *Courtesy of Joyce Sweeney.*

> *Severance Road was a dirt road and over by the turn for Eagle Park and Pheasant Woods in the spring it would be impassable, a mud hole. We used to drive cows down Severance Road every morning after milking to the day pasture* [land owned by Ray Wells in 2009] *and back each night for evening milking, and seldom did we ever hold up a car.*

He also remembers that Route 7 was lined with operating dairy farms from the Winooski border right to Chimney Corners—Button, Parizo, Munson, Collins and Howard Farms were among them.

Both Joyce and Malcolm, like their ancestors, have been active in civic activities. "John [Ebenezer's brother] Severance was said to have held every elected office in the town at one time or another," says Joyce. Malcolm has served on the Planning Commission, and Joyce has been a town assessor, auditor, cemetery commissioner (for more than forty years) and town clerk. Both currently serve on the Colchester Civil Board of Authority, and each has served as town representative in the state legislature. Joyce's and Malcolm's children continue to live in town, so the community is assured of a Severance tradition of helping Colchester grow and prosper for many years to come.

THE COATES FAMILY

And the Island They Treasure

And in future summers,
when we're far away,
Still in spirit we shall wander,
Back to Malletts Bay.
—From "The Camp at Malletts Bay"

It has not always been called Coates Island. The eighty-acre island located off Lakeshore Drive between the state fishing access and the Bayside Bakery originally was called Mather's Head. No one knows why, but that was its name when Thomas Brownell bought it from E.M. Farrington in 1816. Brownell owned it for thirty years, during which time it became known as Brownell's Island, until he sold it to Roswell Newton in 1849. Newton called it Newton's Point and used it as a piece of his 203-acre farm (his farmhouse is now owned by Dale and Shirley Montgomery across from the Malletts Bay Boat Club). Newton also built a hotel called the Malletts Bay House on the land across the road from his home. This house burned down in 1891.

In *Looking at Colchester and Milton* by the Chittenden County Historical Society, Newton's hotel was first identified as Munson's Hotel, and according to Carole Fields's article in the May 1987 issue of the *Colchester Chronicle*, F.F. Gokey built the Malletts Bay Hotel in 1895. The new hotel included a nine-foot veranda, a ballroom, a dining room, water closets and fresh spring water. Gokey ran the following ad in the *Burlington Free Press* on June 30, 1896:

> *Beautiful drive, Malletts Bay Hotel, Five miles from Burlington, three and a one-half miles from Winooski. A first-class dining room, fine fish and game dinners and fine lunches a specialty. Board by the week or month. Excellent boating and fishing. F.F. Gokey, Prop'r P.O. Address Malletts Bay, Vermont.*

The farm was then sold to William D. Munson and Dr. Walter Carpenter in 1867. The land on which the Malletts Bay Hotel stood was held in common, but the rest was divided up, with Carpenter taking the land south of the road (Route 127) and Munson taking the land north of the highway. The island then became known as Munson's Island. In 1872, the island was acquired by William Issac and Adeline Coates, and it still bears that family's name to this day.

"It appears my great-great-grandfather [Issac and wife, Lydia] came from a small town called Ipswich in the County of Clapton near Colchester, England, the nearest big city, in about 1840," says David Coates, who today resides on the island. Their children, Emma and William I. (David's great-grandfather), each married a Thayer. William I. married Adeline Thayer, and they had two children, William and Ida. William married Marie Hanson (David's grandparents), a Swedish citizen who spent summers in Malletts Bay. Ida married John Morrison, a Burlington dentist, and they continued to live in the original family homestead on Route 127.

William I. and Adeline Coates used the island as a farm keeping cows and growing hay. It officially became Coates Island in 1896. "They lived in a small house on the main road [Route 127, Lakeshore Drive] on the other side of what is now Rozzi's Restaurant & Tavern," says David. David grew up in a house built between the Rozzi and Champlain Marina properties that later burned down. "I have pictures of myself and remember that the house was so close to the school [then located across the street from Rozzi's], and it also burned down."

David has tax records from Issac, who appears to have been a surveyor, that indicate a payment of $131 in 1848 to Colchester, Vermont, for property taxes that included four cows and three horses. In 1851, he paid $1,203 in property and personal taxes that included four cows, four horses, four sheep, two hogs and $1,000 (he was the only one to claim cash in his personal inventory tax). In 1856, he used that $1,000 to buy one hundred acres of land (excluding the cemetery and the schoolhouse) on Lakeshore Drive. "That's the first land transaction I can trace," says David.

> *My grandfather moved to the island in 1896 after he and neighbors built the farmhouse. They built the barn the following year. He did everything to make a living…he started the marina, called by the state "Coates Island Marina," but the family always referred to it as the "boat place." He used to conduct fishing trips, for instance, one time he took circus magnate Clyde Beatty out to fish. He would bring his produce from his garden* [on the Rozzi property] *to Burlington to sell. He was a sexton and cemetery commissioner who actually dug graves for five dollars each. He was also a director and stockholder of the Iroquois Power Company that was later sold to Green Mountain Power. He married my grandmother in the farmhouse on the island on August 29, 1903.*

William and Marie Coates on their wedding day in 1903, taken in the farmhouse built by William on Coates Island in 1896. *Courtesy of the David Coates family.*

David remembers his grandfather saying that they got their water from the lake "because if it's good enough for the horses, it's good enough for me."

One of the camps on the island was Camp Winnahkee, a camp for young women. The Native American word *Winnahkee*, "Camp of the Birch Grove," described the well-wooded lot facing the northeast. Another camp run by the same family—the MacVicars—on the opposite shore of the bay called Camp Champlain (now Brown Ledge Camp) was for adolescent boys. In the 1916 brochure explaining its $300-per-season fee, Camp Winnahkee noted, "The cost of a girl's summer in camp should be considered an investment, not an expense, for the benefit she receives there is one which will continue with her throughout her life."

The "outfit" for camp was recommended to be

> *2 blue skirts, 2 pair of bloomers, 1 pair of heavy bloomers, 2 white skirts for Sunday, middy blouses and sweater, 1 pair of high shoes, 1 white hat, 1 blue hat, sneakers or moccasins, dark bathing suits, 1 rubber poncho, 1 bathrobe, 1 raincoat or slicker, high rubbers.*

William Coates (right) fishing with grandsons Jim (left) and Bill off Coates Island, circa 1920s. *Courtesy of the David Coates family.*

Today, David and Margaret Coates and their children summer in the camp originally built about 1900 and have a year-round home in another area of the island. The island is held in trust by David and his siblings, William, James, Gladys and Helen, assuring that it will not be sold. Their father, William Jr., passed away in 1982, and their mother, Minna Aust Coates, died in 1976. There are thirty-five other summer residents (in addition to the Coates family) and three homes, several of which are owned by family members. All of the property is still owned by the Coates-Cadwell Trust, which, in turn, leases out the land.

After 137 years, Coates Island has changed very little. Once you come across the causeway, things are pretty much the same—the farmhouse, the barn, the fields, the camps and campers, the boaters and, of course, the family. The Coates family believes that it is a perfect example of what is possible if a family remains devoted to something it loves and respects.

Many thanks go to David and Margaret Coates for their assistance with this article. David has diligently and painstakingly researched and assembled his family's history on and off the island. For 137 years, the Coates family has owned the island, and David's work in reconstructing his family's history, and the town's, through photos, artifacts, antiques and family memories is an indescribable gift to those yet to come.

THE PORTER FAMILY

Eight Generations on the Land

Joshua Robert Porter is the eleventh generation of Porters in New England and the eighth generation to be living on Porter land in the Porter's Point area of Colchester. Just as there once was a Macrae, a Bean and a Mallett, there was, and is still, a Porter for whom a road or area in Colchester is named.

The first, according to Don Porter Fuller, was Ashbel Porter, whose ancestors were originally from England. Ashbel came up to Colchester from Connecticut with his two sons, Thomas and Elias, about 1804. He established a horse ferry between Porter's Point on Lake Champlain and South Hero, Vermont. "The Porters had been in Vermont before, and right after the Revolutionary War, but not on Porter's Point," says Fuller.

According to Fuller, in September 1814, Thomas took his son, Homer, who was a toddler at the time, on the horse ferry as it was headed to the Battle of Lake Champlain at Plattsburgh, New York. Homer's mother took him off the boat full of troops, but Homer, for the rest of his life, declared that he was the youngest to set out for the Battle of Plattsburgh. "Thomas built a red brick house at Porter's Point, where the horse ferry was based, that was to be his home and also an inn. He also ferried troops in the War of 1812 to the islands," adds Pat Porter, wife of John Porter, who died in 1992. Homer later built a wooden house on Colchester Point Road, where the Airport Park is today. His son, Bernard, raised his family in that house and in a house on North Avenue near the Thayer School. "They spent their winters in a big three-story house in the north end of Burlington. That was the homestead to three Porter brothers and where my husband John's father was raised," remembers Pat.

Bernard died in 1925 and left behind an estate of two farms—one at Colchester and Mills Point that went to his youngest son, Celim John, and the other farm at Porter's Point that went to his oldest son, Homer Bernard. To his three daughters—Ruth Porter Mullen, Helen Porter Kinney and Laura Porter Fuller (Don Fuller's mother)—he left acreage at Colchester Point. "Celim Porter, John's Jr.'s grandfather, was nicknamed 'C.J.' and was born in 1898," says Pat. He raised turkeys and incubated several thousand poults for spring sale. In 1940, according to Ruth Wright, he was elected president of the Vermont Turkey Growers Association.

The Rutland Railroad crossed the Porter land on its way to Mills Point through the Champlain Islands and up to Canada. From the bridge shown here, local children were known to throw turkey eggs at passing trains. *Courtesy of Pat Porter.*

In 1899, Wright notes, Homer and Bernard Porter also

> *sold a strip of land, five rods wide and 25 acres in size to the Rutland and Canada Railroad to complete the section needed to cross the marshes and dunes of Colchester Point, a distance of about two miles.*

Pat remembers that the deed included a stipulation that the railroad agree to drop the Porters off anywhere along the way.

Bernard Porter used Law Island to winter his sheep. "He'd bring them in before the ice defrosted," says Pat. He later sold the island to Claude Watkins. The 350 acres of sand dunes at Colchester Point had been sold much earlier, eventually ending up in the hands of the Hauke family. According to *Look Around Colchester and Milton, Vermont,* a publication of the Chittenden County Historical Society, it was the Haukes who developed the land after purchasing it in the late 1940s. This land had been used previously as a maple sugar grove and an apple orchard. Pat recalls that in this Hauke camp area, there are remains of a French trading post buried under the sand of one of the camps. Pat also remembers hearing the story of moving a three-story house in pieces from Marble Island over the ice by horse-drawn sled to Colchester Point. The house is no longer there, and Pat's sister now lives on the site.

In 1996, Pat and her children—John, Susan and Gill—deeded seventy-nine acres of Porter land to the Lake Champlain Land Trust. "After John died, we started getting offers to sell the land, but we just couldn't do it because he always wanted to keep it open for people to enjoy. The Land Trust was a perfect opportunity to do that," says Pat.

Don and Jane Fuller still own five acres of the family's piece at the tip of Colchester Point and summer there to this day. Brother Jack Fuller only recently (as of 1996) sold similar acreage on the point (just beyond Barney Point). Many members of the Porter family are buried at the Malletts Bay Cemetery on Lakeshore Drive in Colchester.

The Porter legacy will continue through the town's history books with the continued presence of members of the Porter family, as well as in the name of the road leading to their house and the Porter's Point area that is so familiar to local residents.

Thanks to Pat Porter, her daughter-in-law, Tiera Porter, and Don Porter Fuller for their assistance and to Harvey Abbott of the University of Vermont for his help on the land records that concern the Colchester Bog and Sand Dunes.

THE TOWN'S CEMETERIES

A Key to Its Past

Whether you have lived in Colchester for one year, ten years, or all of your life, a walk through one of its cemeteries will quickly and poignantly recall for you its past. The names on the tombstones offer clear clues to the town's history. Perhaps the richest in their definition of our founding families are the three cemeteries located in the village part of town.

MUNSON CEMETERY

The town's first cemetery, this graveyard was originally called the Maple View Cemetery and was "laid out for the purpose of a burying ground," according to Kenneth Degree's article in the winter 1979 *Colchester's Past* newsletter by the Colchester Historical Society. Located on Routes 2 and 7, just south of the intersection with Vermont 127, the cemetery is in good condition and well maintained. There, you will find the family names of Hine, Greenough, Collins and, of course, Munson. The earliest burial date recorded was 1804, with the majority of burials occurring prior to 1860. It has come to be known as Munson's Cemetery, "lying south of William Munson's mill about forty rods to the top of the hill to a large pine tree…containing one acre and nine rods of ground," Degree notes. The name apparently changed to reflect at least six generations of

The Munson Cemetery stone marker of Elijah Wolcott, who served with the Green Mountain Boys in 1778 in the Revolutionary War. He was the first of eight generations of Wolcotts to be buried in Colchester. *Photo by Henry Schaefer.*

Munsons buried there. Inscriptions on the headstones—mostly religious, often melancholy—include the following sentiment, which appeared on two gravestones: "Adieu dear friends, we part in pain. But we may meet and live again" (on the stones of William McEllis, 1819, aged twenty-six years and twenty-three days, and Amasa Hulburd, 1808, twenty-two years old). "The sweet remembrance of the Just / Shall flourish though they sleep in dust" marked Henry F. Gale's headstone (1849, twenty-six years old), and "Who e'er may stop to read my name upon this stone / Think what you mostly need to save a soul undone" appears on the headstone for Rhoda Arnold, wife of Thomas Greenough, who died in 1875 at ninety-nine years of age.

COLCHESTER VILLAGE CEMETERY OR CENTRE CEMETERY

Lying behind the Village Green on Main Street, behind the United Church of Colchester, the Burnham Memorial Library and the Town Meeting House, the Colchester Village Cemetery is the town's largest in terms of both space and burials. The property was sold to the town by Joseph Rhodes in 1848, Degree notes, "to be used for the purpose of a cemetery and no other use whatever and is supposed to contain one acre."

A view from the Colchester Centre or Village Cemetery off Main Street looking at the Baptist Church built in 1861, now a town meeting hall. *Photo by Henry Schaefer.*

Sixteen years later, a petition was brought to the select board to enlarge the burying ground. The parcel contained .88816 of an acre and was bought from Joseph Rhodes for $45.47. Despite the dates of purchase, burials in this cemetery date back to that of Content Bates, buried in 1816. This discrepancy occurs in most of Colchester's cemeteries since it was common practice for towns to take over existing cemeteries either by sale, gift or through abandonment purposes. Family names in this burial ground include: Bates, Bombard, Button, Burnham, Brownell, Cloe, Farnsworth and many members of the Hine, Severance, Thompson, Wolcott and Wright families. There is an average of four burials a year, a practice that, in 2009, has resulted in "the cemetery being just about maxed out," said Sweeney.

Methodist Cemetery

Fanny Munson, daughter of old William Munson, one of the town's earliest settlers and largest landowners, donated the land on which a brick

Methodist church was erected in 1839. The church's location (according to H.F. Walling's 1857 map of Chittenden County) was roughly where the present Claussen's Greenhouse now stands on Main Street, Route 2A. The congregation later moved to its second church, where the Colchester Center Volunteer Fire Station now stands, and the deed for the first parcel was returned to Fanny Munson, according to Kenneth Degree, who has researched the history of the town's cemeteries. Although both the Centre and the Methodist Cemeteries were associated with churches, they were never the property of either church; still, it can be assumed that burial in the early days was reserved for church members and their families.

MALLETTS BAY CEMETERY

A plot with a view is offered at the Malletts Bay Cemetery located on Lakeshore Drive across from the fishing access on beautiful Malletts Bay. "It's almost full," says Joyce Sweeney, a cemetery commissioner since her appointment in 1968. "It appears Julius Dudley was one of the grantors (of at least one-quarter acre) in 1836, but there's no deed," she adds. She also remembers her father saying that a Brownell gave some land. "It's always been a family-oriented cemetery," and according to the headstones, it holds such families as Thayer, Prim, Barstow, Spear, Porter and Coates. In earlier times, this cemetery was known as "North Beach," with the name "South Beach" assigned to the Champlain Cemetery located in the Clay Point area of town.

CHAMPLAIN CEMETERY

According to Ken Degree, the Champlain Cemetery is found "tucked away along Route 2." He says that Levi Peters sold

> *a tract of land...being a part of lot No. 26...to the town in 1832, bounded on the east side by the highway leading from the dwelling house of Levi Peters...to the ferrying place across Lamoil* [sic] *river eight rods*

> *easterly from the northeast corner of the schoolhouse in school district No. 3…containing sixty-four rods of ground.*

Few burials have taken place at this cemetery in recent years, according to Sweeney, so it still has plenty of room.

The Fort Cemetery

This burial ground is still well groomed. Perhaps not as meticulously as it was when there were five thousand troops at the fort, but the grass is cut, the headstones are clean and straight, the trees are tall and well placed and small American flags wave atop the gravestones. It is quiet except for the passing traffic, and it is still within sight of its namesake, Fort Ethan Allen.

The military cemetery (on College Parkway next to the old Fanny Allen Hospital) began when the fort came into being in the late 1890s. It remained a military cemetery until 1963, when the fort was decommissioned, and the General Services Administration transferred ownership to the town. It is no longer necessary for one to be in the military to gain admission to the cemetery. Colchester veterans get a plot free, paying only $200 for perpetual care. A nonveteran Colchester resident pays $350 for the plot plus perpetual care, the same as for the other town cemeteries. Nonresident, nonveteran plots cost $500.

Merrill Cemetery

Located across the road from the entrance to St. Michael's College on College Parkway in the fort area of town, this cemetery was just recently quitclaim deeded over to the college by the town. According to Ken Degree, Merrill ran the tavern, which was later converted into a hospital (Fanny Allen Hospital). The cemetery lay on the boundaries of Arad Merrill's land and the land of Jabez Penniman. Degree writes, "Penniman married Ethan Allen's widow, tended the lime kiln for a spell, and lived in a large house near where St. Joseph's Hall of St. Michael's College now stands." Both Degree and Sweeney say that there is no evidence of a deed to the town or when the cemetery was officially started.

There are three private cemeteries—Religious Hospitallers of St. Joseph Cemetery (on Fanny Allen Hospital land); Holy Cross; and St. Stephen's on Gorge Road by Exit 15, owned by St. Stephen's R.C. Church, Winooski.

The Colchester Cemetery Association, which was incorporated in 1912, operates the three village cemeteries. Three elected cemetery commissioners oversee the other public cemeteries. According to Sweeney, both groups cooperate on the maintenance and other needs of the properties, and there is movement afoot to dissolve the association to allow for one entity to oversee all of the town-owned cemeteries.

Much of the information for this article came from Ken Degree's "Colchester's Cemeteries," Colchester Past *2, no. 1 (Winter 1979) and from a report by University of Vermont graduate student Charles Marchant, who used Degree's work as a reference. Joyce Sweeney, who has been a town cemetery commissioner for forty-one years, also contributed to this article.*

COLCHESTER CHURCHES

Early Houses of Worship Change with Time

Dear old church, spire high,
A hundred years have passed you by,
A hundred years since a faithful few
Envisioned the work a church could do.
—Clara E. Wright, September 11, 1938, from her poem on the centennial of the First Congregational Church, Colchester

Quakers, Protestants (French Huguenots) and Canadian Catholics constituted the religions of the town's early settlers. As new families, primarily from Connecticut, moved to town after the Revolutionary War, the Congregational faith, following the ideals of its spokesman, the Reverend Nathan Perking, took hold. This group, assisted by the Reverend Benjamin Worster of the Connecticut Congregational Home Missionary Society, was the first, according to *Looking at Colchester & Milton*, a booklet by the Chittenden County Historical Society, to organize in Colchester. The group of eight persons "held their first meeting on September 14, 1804, in the 'old plastered schoolhouse' then standing about a mile north of the village on East Road [the area, in fact, was referred to as 'North Colchester']." At the group's next meeting, twenty-one children of the families were baptized. A variety of missionaries and visiting pastors shepherded the group for the next ten years.

A Baptist preacher, here since 1810, organized the Baptist Church Society with a membership of thirteen in 1816. Both churches met where they could until 1814, when a stone schoolhouse was built in the center of the village. The building served as a school, a town hall and a church. "In the summer of 1838, the Congregational and Baptist Societies united to build the brick church, harmoniously shared on alternate Sabbaths for the next 23 years," according to the CCHS booklet. In *A History of the United Church of Colchester 1804–1976*, it is written:

> *In 1838, Joseph Rhodes owned the land on which we are gathered today. Deacon Rhodes' first wife was Mindwell Hine, daughter of Simeon Hine who was the son of William Hine, one of the settlers of Colchester. When Simeon Hine's estate was distributed in 1834, Joseph Rhodes, according to the common law role, came into possession of his wife's portion which consisted of 23 acres lying between what is now our village street, the East Road and the "Indian River," so-called.*

In 1841, Rhodes gave to the congregation and Baptist churches a $4,000 bond as security for a deed to the land on which to build a church. As a condition for the transfer of title, Rhodes asked that an existing building be removed (except for the schoolhouse), that the site be left in good repair and that "said church shall be completed within five years from the above date at a cost of not less than $2,000." The church was built, and in 1840, Joseph and Mindwell Rhodes quitclaimed the land where the church stands to the Congregational and Baptist churches, "each to have an equal interest in the same." In 1848, the town bought "an acre" behind the church for a cemetery.

According to *Colchester, Old Home Week*, "In 1824, the Methodists of this town met and held worship with the Baptists and Congregationalists in an old school house." Kenneth Degree, a historian and former resident, wrote a letter to the *Colchester Chronicle* in 1987 stating that a Methodist church was also later constructed in the village area. He quoted an excerpt from the *1886 History of Chittenden County*: "The first meeting house was built in 1839; it was constructed of brick and cost $1,500. This served until 1869, when the present church edifice was erected; costing $2,500." Degree further offered that the brick church was erected on land donated by Fanny Munson, daughter of William Munson, one of the town's earliest settlers and largest landowners. She sold to the church stewards

> *102 rods of land…it is hereby understood that the said stewards of the church shall build…a house of worship for the Methodist Episcopal*

The Methodist Church, built in 1860. No longer in existence, its demise remains a mystery. *Courtesy of Joyce Sweeney.*

> *Church, 36' broad and 46' length and all finished except inside painting within the space of seven full years.*

Degree examined the 1857 map of Chittenden County and pinpointed the church to be roughly where the present Claussen's Greenhouses now stand. Needing more space by 1860, a second church was built closer to the center of town, where the new fire station is now located. The land from the first church, according to Degree, was then deeded back to Munson. Some gravestones can still be found behind the fire station with dates prior to 1860, but no one is sure of the fate of the building. Degree mused, "Whether the old church was torn down, moved or used for another purpose is likely to remain a mystery."

Not surprisingly, all of the churches were said to have prospered during the Civil War. In 1861, according to the CCHS booklet, with seventy members, "the Baptist Church quit-claimed their interest in the brick church and constructed a church of their own." The white, double-aisled building still appears to be much like it was then. Pew #36, as part of the quitclaim deed, was reserved for the Ebenezer Hine family and their heirs and assigns. As part of the deal, the Congregationalists paid the Baptists $400. Five years later, the Baptists purchased the brick house nearly opposite their church (now the Scanlon House) for their parsonage. With some financial help from a member of the congregation, the Baptists also built a parsonage of brick on East Road in 1863; this building later burned down and was replaced by a frame structure in 1887.

By 1918, committees from both churches (six from the Congregational church, including J. Murray Wright, Mrs. B.E. Severance, Mrs. Alma Wright and William Munson, and six from the Baptist Church, M.E. Thompson, Clark Wright, Ed White, Perry Curtis, Chester Button and Percy Severance) had worked out a one-year trial agreement to have one church, one pastor and one youth society but to hold services in each church for six months of each year. This new church became known as the United Church of Colchester. The two church buildings were used alternately for more than fifty years, with each receiving equal attention. An addition was constructed at the rear of the white Baptist church in 1961 that included a new baptistery. "The original total-immersion font, unusual in this area, was located under the floor of the pulpit; the new font is located under the floor at the rear of the pulpit," the CCHS booklet notes.

In 1971, it was decided that the brick church would become the official house of worship, with the white church used as the Christian Education Building.

On May 16, 1988, the Town of Colchester, in an arrangement to acquire additional land for a planned expansion of the Burnham Memorial Library, entered into an agreement with the United Church of Colchester to purchase land and the white church and adjacent parsonage for $150,000. Payment was to be completed by the fiscal year 1998–99. The white church is currently used as a polling (for District 7-1) and meeting place for civic groups. The parsonage is home to and has been renovated by the Colchester Historical Society. The United Church of Colchester has since expanded and renovated its existing facility.

The former pastor, Brian Kimble, of the United Church reflected in 1996 on the changes the church has made, saying, "New arrivals to the community tended to view the church as the church of another time, another place." The building was in disrepair, and the congregation was unprepared to reach out to the regularly changing population. Further, he says,

> *in a sense, the congregation felt that it had moved into the twentieth century while retaining the charm of the original colonial structure. After almost two hundred years, the church still stands, extending a hand of welcome and help in the name of Christ.*

Other churches serving village residents in more recent times include Our Lady of Grace Church, serving Catholic families since 1956; the original church was constructed in 1959. Father Brian E. Mead, in 1996, said that the church located on Route 2A, Main Street, was expanded and renovated in 1992. The Jehovah's Witnesses Hall, also located off Main Street since 1976, serves its congregation, which represent a broader populace from Chittenden County.

While the religious history of the Malletts Bay area does not quite extend as far back as the village churches, there is little doubt that here, too, many needed to have their spiritual lives nurtured. In 1875, Bishop DeGoesbriand of the Roman Catholic Diocese of Vermont asked Monsignor Jerome Cloarec, pastor of St. Joseph's Church in Burlington, to take spiritual care of the Catholics living in Malletts Bay. Fathers Billon and Lacouture helped him in this effort. According to a history of Holy Cross Church prepared by Bill Hammond in 1986, in 1913 Mr. and Mrs. Richard Lacroix (Cross) donated one acre of land for a building site for a church. In that same year, Father Cloarec planted a wooden cross on the site of the chapel, and since that time the parish has been dedicated to the Most Holy Cross of Jesus Christ.

According to Audrey DeForge, local resident and a Holy Cross Church parishioner, "The church was built with Fr. Cloarec's own funds. He felt it was too hard for the people of Malletts Bay to get to St. Joseph's Church every Sunday for Mass." The total cost for the church, furnished, was $4,987.22,

Father Joseph Joy with a Holy Communion class in 1953 on the steps of Cloarec Hall, built in 1915 as the first chapel to serve Roman Catholics living in Malletts Bay. *Courtesy of Audrey DeForge.*

with parishioners donating what they could, according to Hammond's history. Cloarec Hall became the only Catholic chapel for Malletts Bay residents once it was completed in 1915. "The cornerstone was actually laid in 1914, but it took a year to build," adds Audrey, who says that there were only thirty-five families here at the time.

In the mid-1990s, there was some discussion about taking Cloarec Hall down, after a new church was built and opened in 1967. "It really has no use" was the cry by some, but Audrey DeForge responded, "Cloarec Hall will always be there for something." With her persistence, along with that of others in the church, the building was remodeled instead, including an $8,000 renovation of the steeple. "We had a vote of the congregation to see if they were willing to pay for the steeple repair and they voted two to one in favor—that made me very happy," said Audrey.

To understand Audrey's attachment to Cloarec Hall, one need only hear her speak of her first communion at seven years of age in the chapel, of the baptisms of five of her six children held there, of the weddings of two of her daughters in the chapel, of watching two of her sons serve as altar boys and, more recently, of rejoicing yet again in the same holy place at the baptisms of two of her grandchildren.

> *In 1928, after my mother died, I went to live in Malletts Bay with my maternal grandparents. That was the Bissonette farm that is now a housing area known as Bonanza Park. At that time you would see the same families in church every Sunday—the Beans, Cross family, and the Bosleys.*

After Father Cloarec died in 1920, Father Penders, the chaplain of St. Joseph's Orphanage, took over. He bought the land where the new church now rests and a wooded lot behind the church (some of the property is today used for senior housing). Father Devoy followed until 1945, when Holy Cross became a mission of St. Mark's Church, with Fathers Shortill, Cronin and Tennien serving.

Audrey was not alone in her memories of Cloarec Hall. By 1950, well over one hundred families were being served. In that year, Holy Cross was given the full status of a parish and welcomed Father Joseph Joy as its first pastor. He purchased the land that is now used as a parking lot for Cloarec Hall and the church cemetery. The next building to be added was the rectory, home to Father Joy and those to follow.

"By the end of the 1950s, Holy Cross was crowded with parishioners, especially in the summer. We had masses upstairs and down," says Audrey. In 1962, under the leadership of Father William Hammond, following the untimely death of Father Joy on July 4, 1962, a building committee was formed. In addition to the pledges of parishioners, "we raised money to build the church with dime-a-dip dinners—one a month," remembers Audrey. Groundbreaking for the new church took place on June 5, 1966, and the new Holy Cross Church was completed on July 6, 1967. Father Roger Charbonneau, who began his service to Holy Cross in 1993, continues as its pastor in 2009.

Since then, Cloarec Hall was used for "scouts, Knights of Columbus meetings, AA used to meet here and the Community Christmas baskets were prepared there," according to Audrey. Today, the hall is used for a private day-care facility on its main floor, with the downstairs currently under renovation to accommodate the church's youth group. According to a Holy Cross spokesperson, the youth activities will be open to all young people of the community. Renovations were scheduled to be completed by the summer of 2009.

One cannot help but recall Audrey DeForge's words: "The hall will always be there for something." While most of the parishioners who voted to restore, rather than take down, Cloarec Hall in 1995–96 might not hold the same long-lasting fond memories that Audrey DeForge does, it was their wisdom in wishing to preserve an important part of the legacy of Holy Cross Church that is to be applauded by all Colchester residents.

Other churches in the Malletts Bay area of town include St. Andrew's Episcopal Church on Prim Road, which began holding services at Holy Cross Cloarec Hall in January 1976. It was called the "Colchester Mission," according to St. Andrew's historian Cathie Merrihew, who added that her family and the family of Norma Chicoine were the first parishioners. Several other families joined shortly thereafter, often with Cathie serving as a layperson, along with "supply clergy," before their first priest, Debra Rice, came on duty. The St. Andrew's Episcopal Church on Prim Road opened in the spring of 1984 and is today led by the Reverend Lisette Baxter.

The newest addition to the area is the Malletts Bay Congregational Church, United Church of Christ. Church members began meeting in November 1983 in the Broadacres skating rink on Lakeshore Drive. According to Reverend Mary Nelson Abbott, the church was officially chartered in 1984, exactly one year after the first meeting. The congregation also worshiped in the Malletts Bay School cafeteria before settling into its beautiful white church, with its tall white steeple, on West Lakeshore Drive in 1991.

For more than two hundred years, the spiritual lives of Colchester residents have been nurtured by churches envisioning "the work a church could do." Amen.

THE FORT ETHAN ALLEN AREA

FANNY ALLEN HOSPITAL

"Walking in the Spirit" Since 1894

Since 1894, the Fanny Allen Hospital and the Religious Hospitallers of St. Joseph have been part of Colchester's history and culture. To fully explain how the Fanny Allen Hospital came to be in Colchester, however, one must reach back in time to the early 1600s. It was then that a husband, father of five and tax collector in the small French village of LaFleche "became involved in the care of patients at a pathetically dilapidated home" called Hotel Dieu, according to the the book, *Walking in the Spirit, Fanny Allen Hospital 1894–1994*. This book also tells us more about Jerome le Royer de la Dauversiere, a deeply spiritual man who founded the congregation of women to be known as the Religious Hospitallers of St. Joseph. "The place he envisioned them serving Christ through hospital work was on the yet-unsettled island of Montreal in the wilderness of New France," according to the book's history of the hospital. Mademoiselle Marie de la Ferre assisted him in his work of launching the Hospitallers. A woman of means, she chose instead to pursue a religious life devoted to caring for the poor and sick. She was to become the first of the order that was officially founded on May 18, 1636, under the name of the Daughters of St. Joseph.

Another to join in Jerome le Royer's work was Jeanne Mance, whose name has long been associated with a nurse's training school in Burlington. While not cloistered, Mance was deeply religious and committed to the care of the sick and wounded. After working among the sick in Montreal, she was forced to return to France, where she encountered Jerome Le Royer, with whom she shared a vision of establishing a Hotel Dieu in Montreal. In 1659, this became a reality when three hospital sisters of St. Joseph joined Mance in her journey. She died in the Hotel Dieu, Montreal, in 1673, after struggling in "stark poverty" but "joy in service" for many years.

How the Religious Hospitallers of St. Joseph in Montreal came to Vermont can be attributed to the vision of Bishop DeGoesbriand and his assistant and successor, Bishop John Steven Michaud of Burlington. Realizing the need for a hospital to care for the sick and poor of Vermont and for a caring place to serve as a retirement home for his priests, Bishop deGoesbriand set the task to Bishop Michaud. At this time, the wealthy Fletcher family's fortune was left to its sole heir, Mary Fletcher (considered an invalid as a result of consumption), who "devoted her energies and wealth to establishing the state's first hospital." One of the family's faithful servants was an Irish immigrant named Michael Kelly. Upon the death of Mary (in 1885), he received $10,000. In 1894, Kelly transferred title through Bishop Michaud of "land and premises on southeasterly side of the highway leading from Winooski Park to Essex Junction." On this land was the Merrill Hotel, later sold in 1877 to Frank Dunbar, who changed the name to Dunbar's Hotel. In Kelly's deed, this hotel was to be used as a hospital.

Legend has it that on her deathbed, Mary Fletcher asked Kelly to help establish another hospital to be run by Catholic sisters. Perhaps it was that request, along with his stipulation in the deed that he and his wife receive free lodging in the hospital building whenever they needed it until their death, which prompted the donation. Whatever the reason, in the year 1892, Kelly presented himself to Bishop Michaud with the offer of the property to later become the Fanny Allen Hospital. The Kellys lived on their farm next door to the hospital property until fire destroyed their residence. They then moved into the hospital, where they lived until their deaths in 1907 (Ann Kelly) and 1912 (Michael). It is said that Kelly was also instrumental in establishing St. Michael's College, located across the road from the hospital.

The old Dunbar Hotel in 1917. *From St. Michael's College Archives, Courtesy of the Religious Hospitallers of St. Joseph.*

It was Bishop Michaud who wrote to the Religious Hospitallers of St. Joseph's in Montreal to enlist their help in establishing a hospital in Vermont. The sisters, under Mother Superior Sister Bonneau, deliberated the hardships of such a move. In a letter of response in 1893, the sisters referred to their faith and to the memory of their late sister (Fanny Allen) by saying, "Our dear Sister Allen of sweet and pious memory." The Sister Francis Allen of whom they spoke was none other than the daughter of Ethan Allen (see related article on the amazing story of Fanny Allen's conversion).

On a visit to the site by two of the sisters, they were told that the Penniman Farm on which the Kellys now lived had originally belonged to Fanny Allen's family—yet another connection to this site for the sisters to consider. Before agreeing to come to the hospital, however, the sisters had to be assured of several conditions. They wanted daily Mass and communion, financial support to meet the needs of the sisters and their patients and the preservation of their cloister. Negotiations continued for a while, finally resulting in agreement to the sisters' requests. On May 24, 1894, Sisters Bonneau (to be their mother superior), Perrin, Campbell, Marie-Joseph and Odelia arrived by train in Essex Junction to begin converting Dunbar's Hotel into Hotel Dieu, to later become known as the Fanny Allen Hospital of Vermont.

From the day—May 24, 1894—that the five sisters of the Religious Hospitallers of St. Joseph arrived by train from Montreal to start a hospital in the old Dunbar Hotel, it has been a journey of faith. According to *Walking in the Spirit*, the sisters

> *slept in the attic where, in winter, snow drifted in through the cracks and water froze in the pitchers. Their clothing was patched and every day they swapped shoes from one foot to the other to wear them evenly and to make them last longer. The food was frugal; they raised rabbits for meat for themselves and the patients. They made lye and soap and worked under very primitive conditions.*

The sisters, doctors and nurses used what medical knowledge was available to them, along with plenty of good nursing care, discipline, common sense and faith.

Their first task was to convert the Dunbar Hotel into a hospital. They separated a room that had been a dancehall into private rooms for patients. Another large room was converted into the women's ward, the old office and barroom became the men's ward, a pharmacy was established across the corridor and a doctor's room was provided, along with a kitchen and laundry.

The months after the sisters' arrival were spent cleaning, repairing, renovating and organizing the building. During this time, Bishop Michaud sought and obtained the active cooperation of the medical staff in Burlington and the surrounding areas. In July 1894, the medical society pledged the goodwill and services of the entire medical profession of the neighborhood to work for the success of the hospital. According to a 1988 *Colchester Chronicle* article written by Carole Fields, the community was important in the help it gave to the sisters for renovations, through donations and in other ways. Finally, all was ready for the blessing of the hospital on October 15, 1894, and on this same day, the first patients were admitted. This was exactly 250 years after Jeanne Mance opened the first Hotel Dieu in Montreal in 1644.

"In 1899, the hospital opened its School of Nursing with Mother Renaud, second superior serving as pioneer director. Eight students were enrolled," according to *Walking in the Spirit*. The last class to graduate was in the fall of 1955. A second Catholic hospital called the Bishop deGoesbriand opened in 1924 in Burlington. The Fanny Allen School of Nursing later merged with the deGoesbriand Hospital School and became known as the Jeanne Mance School of Nursing.

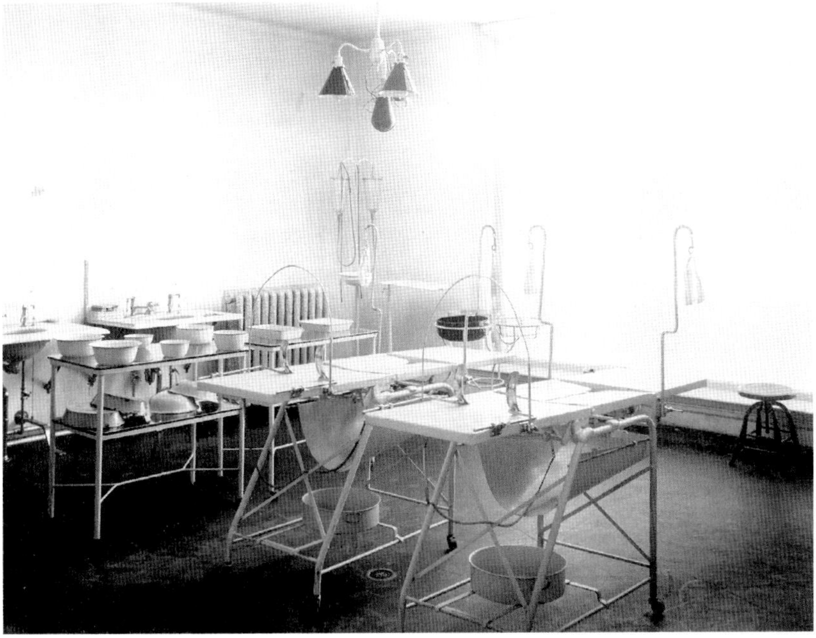

An operating room, circa 1897. *From St. Michael's College Archives, Courtesy of the Religious Hospitallers of St. Joseph.*

A graduating class of the Fanny Allen Nursing School, circa 1920s. *From St. Michael's College Archives, Courtesy of the Religious Hospitallers of St. Joseph.*

The two hospitals shared equipment and services over the years. Fifteen of the Fanny Allen sisters were asked to pack their belongings and move to the deGoesbriand Hospital. While both hospitals were acknowledged for their superior care of patients, both became financially stretched. It was said that the Religious Hospitallers seemed to have adopted Bishop Michaud's motto, "God will provide," as their own. A ladies' auxiliary was formed shortly after the Depression started, and in 1934 the Fanny Allen Hospital Aid Association was started. This association has, over the years, successfully raised money for the hospital. The state's first blood/plasma bank was established at the hospital in 1942, along with the first hospital volunteer service.

Because of a controversy in the 1950s over the future of the two hospitals, in 1956 a plan developed by then Bishop Ryan recommended that Fanny Allen be converted into an eighty-four-bed nursing home. At the same time, a proposal to sell deGoesbriand to the University of Vermont was being considered. With the death of Bishop Ryan, resolution of the situation was left to the new bishop, Most Reverend Robert F. Joyce. Initially, Bishop Joyce was intent on closing Fanny Allen as a community hospital. At the request of Sister Annunciata, superior and administrator, the board of directors and Bishop Joyce transferred the ownership of the hospital to the Religious Hospitallers of St. Joseph. Under Sister Annunciata's leadership, the federal government certified the hospital for Medicare patients. She also led a successful fundraising campaign with a long-range plan to build a new hospital to replace the original wooden structure (the old Dunbar Hotel), which did not comply with accreditation standards. Once again, the private sector rose to the occasion and, with the guidance of Douglas Cairns, helped raise substantial sums of money.

In 1957, the sisters established the Fanny Allen Memorial School of Practical Nursing. Groundbreaking for a new Fanny Allen Hospital took place in 1967. In 1972, groundbreaking for the second phase of the hospital's modernization took place. This new wing was called St. Joseph's Pavilion; it opened in 1973. In 1976, the third phase—housing the laboratory, an X-ray department and outpatient and emergency departments—was completed, and in 1977, a chapel connecting the sisters' convent to the hospital was opened.

In 1995, the Fanny Allen Hospital merged with the University Health Center, Medical Center Hospital of Vermont, in an alliance with the University of Vermont, leasing the entire property to Fletcher-Allen Health Care. An article in the lease agreement specified that Fanny Allen was to retain its Catholic identity and presence, respecting and promoting the mission, heritage and values of the Religious Hospitallers of St. Joseph. In 1997, an extensive renovation project was undertaken for services, including a walk-in care center, X-ray services (including CT scanning and ultrasound), ambulatory surgery and an inpatient comprehensive rehabilitation center and outpatient rehabilitation therapies. The center was opened in 1999.

In 2008, the Religious Hospitallers of St. Joseph transferred sponsorship responsibilities to Covenant Health Systems, a New England–based Catholic health system with headquarters in Lexington, Massachusetts. The Fanny Allen Corporation Board of Directors established the Fanny Allen Corporation Foundation under the leadership of Sister Irene Duchesneau as executive director. Partnering with more than fifty organizations and agencies sharing a mutual commitment to improve the quality of life and promote healthier communities throughout Vermont actualizes the mission of the sisters.

In reflecting on the hospital's future, Dick Mazza, a former president of the Fanny Allen Association, said in 1997, "It was successful because of all the Sisters involved—they offered that personal touch that is difficult to replace. When I was a patient here in 1969, they just about came in at night and tucked you into bed."

Given the resolve of Sister Irene Duchesneau and the spirit that walks the hallways of the Fanny Allen Hospital campus, that personal touch of the Religious Hospitallers of St. Joseph might just help determine the health care culture of tomorrow—we'll just have to keep the faith!

Sister Irene Duchesneau assisted with this article in 1997 and graciously provided the updates in 2009.

Fanny Allen: A Revelation

If there is a name profoundly associated with Vermont, it is that of the Allen family. Specifically, it is that of the brothers Ethan and Ira Allen, each of whom had a distinct influence on the early history of the state. Ethan, the more popular leader of the Green Mountain Boys who captured Fort Ticonderoga from the British forces in 1775, was the dashing and daring one who later attacked Montreal and was defeated and captured. Ira is best known for helping to establish the state of Vermont in 1791 and founding the University of Vermont that same year; coincidentally, he later became "Clark" of Colchester (or its town clerk) in 1774.

From this unlikely family of rascals and radicals came Frances Margaret Allen, born in 1784. Her mother, Francis Montressor Buchanan Allen, a widow from southern Vermont, was Ethan's second wife after his first had passed away. They came to Burlington in 1787 and lived on a farm (now the Ethan Allen Homestead on the Intervale). Following the death of her father in 1789, when Fanny was only four years of age, her mother married a man named Jabez Penniman. Penniman, a physician, cared deeply for Fanny. Both father and stepfather, however, shared a disdain and distrust of religion. Ethan was believed to have been an atheist. According to David Bryan's brochure, *The Life of Sister Fanny Allen, RHSJ*, Allen resented "the clergy of his day whom he regarded as insufficiently attached to the common man." In an article on Jabez, Barry Boss notes that Fanny's stepfather "had little use for the rigid Puritan Christianity" found among his Vermont neighbors. For Fanny to consider herself agnostic was not an unexpected outcome.

Fanny wished, however, to go to Montreal to continue her education, intending specifically to learn French, and she persuaded her parents to send her to the convent school of the Sisters of the Congregation de Notre Dame. Before leaving, however, her mother insisted that she be baptized in the Protestant faith; the Reverend Daniel Barber of New Hampshire did the honor. Fanny was then twenty-three years of age and engaged to a young man, Archibald Hyde, who was about to graduate from the University of Vermont. Once at school in Montreal, Fanny gave the good nuns a difficult time with her "mockery of religion," and the sisters even considered sending her back to Vermont. She had one ally she was fond of, however, and legend has it that this sister one day asked Fanny to place some flowers at the altar in preparation for the Feast of St. Mary's Nativity. Wishing to please her favorite sister, Fanny approached the sanctuary gate, but her feet became rooted and she could move no further. She tried and tried but was unable to budge. The story goes that she fell to her knees in prayer and thereafter took instruction in the faith. She was later baptized as a Catholic. It was not long after, despite the protestations of her family and fiancé, that she would begin her pursuit to become a nun.

Fanny's service to God as a nun is also an intriguing story. It stems from an experience she had at twelve years of age while walking along the Winooski River. She became frightened by something in the water, and a passerby "saved" her by helping her away from the river's edge.

Sister Fanny Allen, 1784–1819. *Photo by Inge Schaefer.*

She shared the experience with many and continued to look for the "stranger who rescued her," but to no avail. One day, as she was visiting the Hotel Dieu Hospital, she saw a painting of the Holy Family. In that painting, she found the man who had saved her on that day thirteen years before—it was Saint Joseph. She took this as a sign that she was to stay at the Hotel Dieu. It took another year before she was accepted as a novice at the hospital. Needless to say, as Bryan notes, her decision "rocked the family," but by the time she took her final vows, her stepfather had endowed the convent with enough money to cover Fanny's expenses, and the profession ceremony included many of her Vermont family and friends. Fanny worked alongside her sisters in the hospital serving the sick and, during the War of 1812, tending the wounded and injured soldiers. Bryan writes, "The Hotel Dieu, which had tended her father's wounded soldiers in the attack of 1775, was again flooded with suffering men to whom Fanny could minister in either language."

Sister Francis Allen died of a lung infection at the young age of thirty-five. She never saw the hospital that carries her name to this day. She is buried in the chapel of the Hotel Dieu on St. Paul Street in Montreal, just a few feet away from the painting of St. Joseph, whom she so revered. Her sisters of the Religious Hospitallers never forgot their beloved sister in faith, however. When Bishop John Michaud called upon them to serve the sick in Vermont, they recalled Sister Fanny and considered the offer. When they realized that the land on which the hospital was to be established had originally belonged to Fanny's family, they were further convinced to come to Vermont. In their acceptance letter to Bishop Michaud, they recalled the first American nun of their order: "our dear Sister Allen of sweet and pious memory."

FORT ETHAN ALLEN: FROM MILITARY PARADES TO RUGBY

By John Gant

I want to take you back in time. The year is 1890. The United States has grown to forty-three states with the addition to the union of North Dakota, South Dakota, Montana, Washington and Idaho. Ellis Island has opened to handle the rush of immigrants to the land of opportunity. The Sioux have been defeated at the Battle of Wounded Knee in South Dakota, signaling the end of the Indian Wars. Benjamin Harrison is our president, and former Vermont governor Redfield Proctor is the secretary of war.

The United States was emerging as a world power, and with this came the need for a well-organized, standing army. The relatively unprotected northern border emerged as a major concern. This area had been a major concern since Samuel de Champlain first challenged the Iroquois here in 1609. Lake Champlain was of strategic military importance. It had been the corridor of battle in previous wars and offered a direct water route to the Great Lakes and America's heartland. Proctor began to devise plans for a permanent military base in the state. A fort near the lake would allow a cavalry unit the ability to make a "prompt dash upon the canal system of Canada…to prevent the British from sending gunboats into the Great Lakes" (even though history would show that it was never needed for this purpose).

The defeat of the Sioux meant the imminent closing of the many small army forts scattered throughout the western states. The army wanted to concentrate its troops in larger encampments for economy of supply and training, as well as to distribute the soldier "more generally among the states." In 1885, there were seventy-five forts west of the Mississippi and fewer than a dozen, all small, east of the Mississippi. Vermont representative John Stewart brought the issue to the House. Vermont senator Justin Morrill took it to the Senate. The legislation failed to pass in both houses, despite a general agreement of the need for protection of the northern frontier. In 1891, Proctor resigned his cabinet post to fill a vacant Senate seat. His bill passed in the Senate on March 8, 1892. The House bill had a harder time but finally passed (after the word "Vermont" was removed completely from the bill). One of the strongest objectors to the fort was a representative from Kansas who wanted the fort to be built in his state, claiming that Kansas could feed the troops more cheaply and offer them better weather.

The bill that finally passed stipulated that the land had to be donated free of charge to the United States. Six hundred acres was needed (only 138 acres for the actual fort itself). Dr. W. Seward Webb of Shelburne contributed $8,500, and another $3,000 came from the Central Vermont Railroad. The remaining $10,000 was gathered at a meeting at the Burlington YMCA in September 1892 from pledges and subscriptions.

The government named the fort "Ethan Allen" after the leader of the Green Mountain Boys. Coincidentally, Ethan's brother Ira had once owned some of the property. The original phase of construction was bid in March 1893. The bid was awarded to James McFarren of West Troy, New York, for $99,000 and included barracks for 120 men, a guardhouse, two stables, two double officers' quarters, a bakery, a storehouse and a scale

The cavalry at Fort Ethan Allen. *Courtesy of Ann Wetzel.*

house. The second phase of construction started that same year, and it provided the hospital, blacksmith's forge and two double noncommissioned officers' quarters.

The fort was not here to defend Vermont against Canada. Canadian military officials were invited to the fort from the beginning, including Captain Lee of the Royal Military Academy in Kingston, who visited the fort in 1895. This is also one of the main reasons why the fort was not constructed in the Highgate/Swanton area as originally planned. The other reason was that this spot offered better access to the rail system. In 1894, the state legislature authorized the purchase of land for use as a National Guard campground alongside the fort. This area was first called the state reservation and then was named after successive governors until 1945, when it became Camp Johnson.

Troops C, E, F and G of the Third U.S. Calvary moved into their new home in September 1894. They came in two trains; the first held the horses and the other carried the men and baggage. They came directly from Chicago after putting down Pullman Railroad strike rioting. They had seen as much service as any command in the army from the Texas border to Fort Riley, Kansas, and from the opening of the Cherokee Strip to Chicago, Illinois.

Local citizens were not disappointed with the growth of the fort. Most of the building materials were from Vermont, including Essex's own Drury bricks and limestone from a quarry east of Route 7, as well as Vermont granite and blue slate. There was also a need for lumber, hay, grain and other Vermont supplies. Citizens could see Troop F, a mounted exhibition drill team and the pride of the U.S. Cavalry. It performed throughout the Northeast while stationed at the fort. By the end of 1895, the government had spent $400,000 on the post, including $7,000 to purchase about 190 acres between the front of the fort and the Winooski River on the other side of Route 15.

The fort became an integral part of the community, providing entertainment for the troops and townspeople alike. This included Sunday afternoon bandstand concerts and polo, baseball and football matches, as well as horse and pistol shows.

The Seventh Field Artillery Camp, 1928. *Courtesy of Greg Dirmaier.*

In 1898, on the eve of the Spanish American War, the Third Cavalry was transferred out of the fort, and the fort became a mobilization point for the Vermont National Guard. The guard was recruited to maximum strength. Twelve companies from the fort left by train but were detained in Georgia and never saw service in Cuba. A small burst of expansion happened in 1897–98 resulting in two more cavalry stables, band barracks, a double guardhouse, three buildings for housing officers and one for noncommissioned officers, a storehouse and the bandstand. By 1904, the fort had grown in size from 600 acres to 761.08 acres. Additional expansion in 1904 added more officers' quarters, a barracks for single officers, four barracks for enlisted men, an addition to the bakery, five artillery stables, the post exchange, several shops, a steel water tower (no longer standing), three storehouses and three oil houses. Electricity came in 1905 (natural gas had been used before), ending the need to pump water by hand. The fort was now complete.

The plans used for the fort were standard from the quartermaster general's office and were identical to other forts built at the same time, such as Fort Logan in Colorado, the Presidio in California and Fort Crook in Nebraska. The dominant arch style is Colonial Revival. Details include keystone lintels, denticulate cornices and Palladian windows. The military's social structure is expressed in the fort's plans by having the officers in the front row, noncommissioned officers near the front and on the sides, enlisted men behind the officers and stables in the rear.

The famous "Buffalo Soldiers" of the Tenth Cavalry were among the many troops stationed here. This unit of black soldiers saw service in the Spanish-American War and the Texas border disputes and were stationed in Colchester from 1909 to 1913. This regiment was also General John J. Pershing's first command. During 1916, a great many of the troops were reserve officer training corps cadets from Norwich and the Massachusetts University (Cavalry), Harvard and Yale (Field Artillery). During World War I, the fort was the scene of much activity over a four-year period when eight thousand troops were trained there. During this time, technology and warfare had changed; motorized vehicles and tanks changed the role of the cavalry soldier forever. Many of the stables were converted to garages reflecting this change.

A small number of horse soldiers remained at the fort. They participated in parades and occasionally in guard duty. In 1934, the last of the heavy draft horses was sold, and the stables were redesigned for automobiles. In 1927, fort troops played a dominant part in rescue and supply after the great flood. During this time, the parade grounds were used briefly as a runway for

Fort Ethan Allen, circa 1921. *Courtesy of Frank von Turkovich.*

the daily mail plane. Presidents Theodore Roosevelt and William McKinley visited the post. From 1902 to 1959, the base had its own post office.

In the 1930s, congressional spending on the military was greatly reduced. The field artillery units had dry-run practices at the Underhill Firing Range all year, except for one week, during which they could use live rounds. One month, the soldiers were not paid because Congress failed to pass a budget. During the same time, the fort provided Depression relief in the New Deal years. It was headquarters for the Vermont Civilian Conservation Corp (CCC) from 1933 to 1938. Temporary barracks were built to provide housing for the trainees prior to their assignment to one of thirty-seven CCC companies.

In anticipation of possible involvement in World War II, the fort saw another intense construction period. In 1940, Congress allocated $1 million for the construction of nearly one hundred wooden buildings (used to house 40 to 65 men each) for National Guard troops in the Camp Olympia area (between Camp Johnson and the fort—no longer there). Nineteen mess halls were constructed to serve 170 men each. Permanent structures were built at Camp Johnson in 1950 to house the new headquarters of the Vermont National Guard.

The Seventh and Thirty-third Field Artillery Units left for Fort Devons, Massachusetts, in 1941. Twenty-three hundred national guardsmen from New York and New Jersey replaced them. More quarters were built, along with numerous garages and repair shops. Over the next two years, more than five thousand men from all over the country arrived at the fort, marking the peak of its military role. Just three years later, in 1944, it would be declared inactive. The fort continued to serve as a supply depot, but many of the buildings were allocated to the Public Housing Authority for civilian occupancy.

The 134th Fighter Interceptor Squadron of the Vermont Air National Guard arrived in 1951. Later that year, the U.S. Air Force took control of the fort and it was renamed "Fort Ethan Allen Air Force Base." In 1958, $4.7 million of a $13.5 million Goose missile program was allocated to the fort. After spending $1 million, the project was cancelled. In 1960, despite much local and state protest, the air force announced the closing of the air base. Options discussed for the use of the fort included a missile stockpile area, a jet repair and maintenance center, a cold weather missile research center, an international refugee center and a Peace Corps training center. Nothing feasible developed; thus, in 1961, 787 acres of the fort were returned to and disposed of through the General Services Administration.

New owners included the state, which purchased twenty acres; forty acres each went to St. Michael's College (SMC) and the University of Vermont. Students from Craftsbury used the buildings as temporary classrooms after their school burned in 1961. A minimum of new construction has taken place since then. The three largest construction efforts included UVM's married student housing area, Gero Brothers Moving building and the ETV Studios. A former historic riding hall owned by St. Michael's College has been converted into the Elley-Long Music Center and is leased to the Vermont Youth Orchestra for just one dollar a year. Fires have claimed SMC's Sullivan Hall (used for ROTC) and Firetech's buildings on Hegeman Avenue (rebuilt and reopened in 1995 after a restoration project that held to historic structure standards allowing the building to be listed on the National Historic Register) and at 1302 Ethan Allen Avenue. In 1991, Governor Howard Dean officially broke ground for the rehabilitation of Officers' Row, with all seventy-seven units renovated and occupied by 1995. The parade grounds are now used by the Burlington Rugby Club for their games. Children romp on a playground in one corner of the field and play soccer in view of the parade ground reviewing stand, which saw much of what is contained in this history of Fort Ethan Allen.

Fort Ethan Allen has stood now for a full century and then some. It has retained most of its cultural and architectural integrity, despite all of the changes that have taken place. Today, new occupants of old buildings seem to be energized by all that has settled in the walls and floors of their buildings.

They strive to retain what legacy they can of the old post and to keep for us all the spirit that is Fort Ethan Allen.

Years ago, when the Colchester News Magazine *ran a historical series of articles on the town, the thought of presenting such a perspective of Fort Ethan Allen was daunting. Where to begin? Information on the fort area of Colchester located between Winooski and Essex Junction on College Parkway was everywhere and nowhere in particular. The name of John Gant surfaced as someone who had lived in one of the houses on Officers' Row and had developed an interest in the fort's history. As a result of his interest, he developed a lecture/slide presentation on the history of the fort, and that is the narrative you have just read. John Gant credits the following sources for his information: National Register of Historic Places of the United States Department of the Interior;* Vermont History, The Proceedings of the Vermont Historical Society *XXXV, no. 1 (January 1967);* Look Around Colchester and Milton, Vermont *(Chittenden County Historical Society, 1975); and Ruth Wright's* Colchester, Vermont Ice-Cap to Interstate *(1963). Thanks also to Ann Wetzel and Frank von Turkovich for the photos they contributed.*

St. Michael's College

From Reaping Corn to Sowing Minds

What was once a barren eighteen-acre farm in Colchester known as the Michael Kelly property has now become one of the finest colleges in the Northeast, according to recent (1997) surveys in *Money Magazine* and *U.S. News and World Report.*

According to *St. Michael's College: A Brief Chronicle* by Joseph T. Popecki, "Jean-Baptist Muard of Sens in France was inspired in 1841 to found a community of diocesan missionaries that he called quite simply, 'the Priests of the Sacred Heart." Two years later, with Father Peter Boyer, his friend from seminary days, he accepted the offer of his archbishop to take up residence in the former Cistercian Abbey at Pontigny. This marked the time and place of the birth of the Society of St. Edmund. As Muard decided to follow yet a different drummer in his search for spiritual development, Boyer took over as superior, and in 1852, when the community was declared a diocesan religious institute, he gave it the unbelievably lengthy name "Society of the

St. Michael's College logo.

Fathers and Brothers of Saint Edmund, Oblates of the Sacred Heart of Jesus and the Immaculate Heart of Mary." When the French government began to eliminate religious orders by appropriating their properties in the late 1800s, the society decided that Canada "might be a good place to look for a new home." The archbishop of Montreal suggested that it contact Bishop deGoesbriand in Burlington, Vermont. DeGoesbriand offered them a small parish in Keeler's Bay near Lake Champlain.

Though the Canadian parish was considered almost in exile, the society had at least established a foothold in the New World. Meanwhile, in Europe, the society moved to Hitchin, England, where it established St. Michael's School. In 1924, the European chapter voted to dissolve, but with the support of the American hierarchy, the society reestablished a generalate in Swanton, Vermont. Popecki writes:

> *With the assistance of Mother Renaud* [superior at Fanny Allen Hospital] *and Fr. Jean Audet* [pastor of St. Francis Xavier parish

Members of the Society of the Fathers of St. Edmund on the campus of St. Michael's College, started in 1904. *Courtesy of St. Michael's College.*

> in Winooski], *arrangements were made to purchase the Michael Kelly property in Colchester "where the Society intends to establish a college and the principal house novitiate.*

Officially, the college was incorporated in March 1903 as St. Michael's Institute. About this time, the Holy See requested the community to shorten its name to the "Society of the Fathers of St. Edmund."

With a line of credit of $12,000 from the Burlington Savings Bank, construction on the first building began, and, Popecki notes, in "September of 1904, the building was dedicated and opened to the first 35 students, 28 of whom were boarders." Recognizing the value of receiving both a practical and liberal education, the courses of studies were both classical and commercial and taught in both English and French. Reverend Michael

Cronogue, SSE (Society of St. Edmund), director of the college's ministry, said, "The goal of the Edmundites when they established this institution was to provide a quality Catholic education for people in Vermont who could not afford to go elsewhere."

Reverend Armand Prevel was named the first president and superior of the community. Tuition was $143. As its second president, Father Salmon incorporated the school as St. Michael's College in 1913. Father Edmund Total, the next SMC head, bought several neighboring properties, enlarging the campus. Under Father William Jeanmarie (whose family would later simplify their name to that of Jemery, now used on Jemery Hall), the Reynolds property was acquired, along with a house now called Prevel Hall. A 160-acre parcel (the Xavier Seguin Farm) across Route 15 was later acquired through the generosity of local clergy, giving the college a 225-acre campus. According to Popecki:

> *As the Great Depression afflicted the nation, Fr. Eugene Alliot was elected president. SMC hosted the first winter carnival at its new ski jump in 1932. Other happenings of note: the first systematic practice teaching program was inaugurated in cooperation with Cathedral High School in Burlington; intramural football was dropped* [for the first time] *and the Sisters of Saint Martha arrived from Canada to assume domestic duties at the college.*

In 1934, Reverend Leon Gosselin became the first graduate of the college to become president. In 1942, the college moved to a year-round schedule, with Jerry Durick managing the summer session, an academic department that would substantially affect the academic visibility for the college both during and after World War II. Elsa Sichel, who had earned an enviable reputation in the field of biology, became the first full-time woman teacher at the college. At the end of the summer of 1945, SMC graduated its first laywoman (Eileen McGinley) through its summer session program.

After World War II, the college boomed structurally. The influx of ex-GIs caused Reverend Daniel P. Lyons to negotiate with the U.S. government for twenty-two buildings from Fort Ethan Allen. These buildings were relocated to the main campus and housed the convent, infirmary, classrooms and library. They have all been demolished, except for what was then the library and is now the Klein Academic Center, serving as a student resource center (career planning, resume writing, peer tutoring, etc.).

Founders Hall of St. Michael's College. *Courtesy of St. Michael's College.*

In 1954, President Moriarty implemented a radical new curriculum, again dropped football (after an unbeaten season) and inaugurated the Program of English for Foreign Students. Don and Joanne Rathgeb, who would take drama and theatre arts to new heights at the college, joined the faculty in 1961. Then vice-president Lyndon Johnson visited the campus in 1963. SMC's first lay president, Bernard Boutin, was installed in 1969 amidst student unrest involving "parietals" (the right of the male students to have female visitors). Also in 1969, Boutin asked Don Sutton and Tom Powers to form a public safety (rescue) service, and baseball great Jackie Robinson visited the campus.

It was not until the 1970s, however, that the campus took on its present appearance. Richard DiVenere, associate vice-president for alumni relations and development, came to SMC in 1973 and has seen many of the changes. "In thinking of the biggest difference since I have been here…I think structurally the campus has changed dramatically," said DiVenere.

> *When I came here there was no McCarthy Arts Center and no real academic building for classes. The campus has improved tremendously since then; the facilities have been upgraded from marginal to current state-of-the-art.*

St. Michael's not only changed structurally in the 1970s, but its student body changed significantly as well. In the spring of 1971, the trustees of the college approved the admission of women. Dr. Carey Kaplan, an English professor, came to SMC in 1972, one year after the college went coeducational. She said that the main reason for accepting women was very simple: money. "At first, women were very excited, but once they arrived there was a mixed bag of reactions, ranging from delighted to appalled," said Kaplan. That may have been due to the fact that there were only thirty women among sixteen hundred men.

On October 3, 1975, the board of trustees named Edward L. Henry the thirteenth president of the college. Under Henry, a learning center and an apartment-style dormitory were added. He established a pilot program to encourage experimental curricular projects and a grants program, and he expanded the international student program.

Today, the school is completely wired with computer technology and has just finished a phase of building acceleration under immediate past president Dr. Paul J. Reiss, who was elected fourteenth president in 1986. Under Dr. Mark vanderHeyden, SMC's fifteenth president, the campus expanded to include the Hoehl Welcome Center, the Duffy All-Weather Playing Field, three residence halls and the Sutton Fire and Rescue Station. His most significant academic advance was the college's acceptance into the highly prestigious national honor society Phi Beta Kappa, and he broadened the college's international perspective and its community outreach into the wider New England world. Dr. Jack Neuhauser now leads the college.

Today, there are approximately 2,000 students from thirty-three states and thirteen countries, with 150 faculty members. The student-faculty ratio is 12:1. With a mission "to contribute through higher education to the enhancement of the human person and to the advancement of human culture in the light of the Catholic faith," the school curriculum is based on liberal arts, with thirty major fields of study. It has a Phi Beta Kappa chapter on campus and is annually ranked among the top "Best National Liberal Arts Colleges" by the *U.S. News and World Report.* It is also included in the Princeton Review's *Best 368 Colleges* guidebook. The Applied Linguistics Department enrolls students from over forty countries, and its well-known master's degree program in "Teaching English to Speakers of Other Languages" is highly acclaimed. The St. Michael's Playhouse brings professional summer theatre to the community and includes internships for its students.

A school rich in tradition that moves into the future with conviction and promise, St. Michael's College remains a source of deep pride to the community in which it resides.

This article was originally written in December 1997 by Bryan P. Goodchild, a junior majoring in journalism at SMC. Historical quotes were generally taken from Saint Michael's College, Colchester, Vermont—A Brief Chronicle *by Joseph T. Popecki, archivist and director of SMC Library Emeritus, September 1994. Updates on the college were provided by SMC's Public Relations Office, with special thanks to Dr. Buff Lindau.*

LANDMARKS I

Gone, but Not Forgotten

COLCHESTER LIGHTHOUSE

Splendid Isolation

In a pamphlet entitled *Life in the Colchester Reef Lighthouse: The Life of a Lighthouse Keeper* issued by the Shelburne Museum, author Gordon P. Manning graphically describes not only the lighthouse but also the isolation that existed for those tending it. Day-to-day activities were chronicled in the logs kept by lighthouse keeper Albert Hunter, and a separate article excerpting his writings follows.

If you are standing on the Colchester Causeway (found on Colchester Point Road in Malletts Bay) and looking out toward the Adirondack Mountains, you will see an automatic beacon atop some rocks, just about a mile opposite Colchester Point. That beacon replaced the Colchester Reef Lighthouse and marks the spot where it once stood. It is in the center of a group of three treacherous shoals, Manning writes, "which in effect, rimmed the northern approach to Burlington harbor." The federal Lighthouse Service completed it in 1871, likely following the floundering of several early sailing craft and towboats on their way to Burlington. Water traffic was heavy, despite the danger of islands and reefs in this area.

A clue as to the significance of Lake Champlain is its Indian name, which meant, "the-lake-that-is-the-gateway-to-the-country." Freight and passengers traveled from St. Johns and Rouses Point south to Whitehall, New York (the birthplace of the U.S. Navy). Barges with tugs, schooners, pin plats, rafts and, later, steamboats filled the lake, with early settlers preferring navigation to road building. It is said that the lumber trade in the late 1800s alone created sufficient traffic in this area to warrant the building of the lighthouse. The shoals, composed of Colchester Reef, Colchester Shoals and Hogback Reef, presented little concern during a clear day—particularly Colchester Reef, which could be seen a few feet above water. In foul weather, with adverse winds and darkness, even experienced skippers became unsure of their exact locations.

The decision to build the lighthouse was made in 1869. "The Lighthouse Service decided to run a contest among architects and engineers for the best design of the future lighthouse," Manning wrote. Interestingly, despite being a national contest, the winner was from Burlington, Vermont—Albert R. Dow, a graduate engineer of the University of Vermont. His drawing is on display in the lighthouse, which was moved to the Shelburne Museum fifty-six years ago. As can be seen on the plans, the dwelling was quite adequate and modern for its day. The building's twenty-five-foot-square, post-and-beam frame, foundation, roof and tower are pegged and bolted together and secured with one-and-a-half-inch-thick iron rods. The roof was an ornamental mansard, and scrolled window frames were typical of the French Second Empire style. It had four bedrooms upstairs; a kitchen, sitting room and toilet room downstairs; and a basement. A four-foot walkway surrounded the house. While there was no central heat or furnace, a coal range sufficed for cooking and warmth in the kitchen, with the Lighthouse Service supplying the coal. Portable brass oil lamps using kerosene were also supplied by the landlord and provided light in the evening. A pitcher pump in the kitchen directly into the lake supplied the water, and a chemical toilet situated in a closet near the front door solved the plumbing needs of the keepers. Completing the package was a twelve-foot dory used to transport the keeper and his family back and forth to the shore.

The building was completed in 1871 at a cost of $20,000. Additional costs were incurred when the foundation was damaged in its first winter and in 1873 during a "fierce storm." According to the website Lighthousefriends.com, the foundation was replaced with riprap at a cost of $5,000.

The keeper was to be in the lighthouse during the navigation season, from April to January, leaving only for supplies, and even then someone was expected to be on duty. The light in the lamp was to be lit at sunset nightly and kept burning until sunrise (it was visible for eight miles). In times of fog, a fog bell was rung and kept going (automatically, based on a clockwork mechanism similar to a grandfather's clock) until the fog was lifted. According to Manning, a daily log was to be kept "recording weather, wind velocity, times of lighting and extinguishing the lamp, visitors, and any unusual or important events."

Maintenance of the entire operation was also his duty. Because of the significance of this responsibility, the Lighthouse Service provided the necessary tools and equipment to properly do the job. The first keeper was Herman Malaney, Manning notes, who quickly realized that the

> *brilliance of his lighthouse beam depended in large measure upon how clean the magnifying glasses were that reflected the light out across the water…one fingerprint could cut down measurably on its visibility.*

His second most important chore was the cleanliness of the heavy plate-glass sides of the lamp room so as not to cut down on the intensity of the beam before it even left the lighthouse. Soot from the oil, flies, moths and spider nests all contributed to the need to regularly clean the equipment.

Walter Button, the next keeper in 1882, brought along his family, which suited the service just fine since it meant that there would be someone on duty—at no extra charge—at all times. One interesting scenario surfaced, however. Harriet Button was to have a baby during the frozen winter. Always resourceful, Walter reasoned that if the baby came before the lake froze, old Dr. Hawley from Burlington (eight miles away) could come by horse-drawn wagon quickly enough, and Walter could then ferry him over in the rowboat. Better still would be if the lake froze over because then the doctor could manage the distance on his own, walking the last mile across the ice if necessary. The best-laid plans, however, unfolded on a cold evening in January, when the lake lay between open water and solid ice. Based on a prearranged signal of ringing the foghorn in the event of the oncoming birth, Walter had confidence that somehow the doctor would manage to get to them in time. When the doctor arrived at the shore, it was almost dark. He decided to chance the flimsy ice. Suddenly, following a loud, cracking noise, the doctor, along with Walter's reliable assistant, found himself caught on an ice cake drifting "steadily out to sea." As it broke up, they had to jump from one piece to the next, "all the while being blown northward." Walter watched the men on the ice cake, unable to do anything for them. Myrtle Edna Button was born that night; she was their fifth child. Dr. Hawley and the assistant drifted seemingly forever before coming up on

The Colchester Lighthouse, built in 1871 and decommissioned in 1933. It now rests at the Shelburne Museum. *Courtesy of the Shelburne Museum.*

the shores of South Hero, a good three to four miles away. Details of this experience, as well as the Buttons' gardening successes, the antics of their five children living in a lighthouse and other interesting stories, may be found in Manning's pamphlet, available at the Burnham Memorial Library on Main Street in Colchester.

Button's son, Chester, took over, after seventeen years of service by his parents, in the year 1901. He and his wife had seven children—all wisely born onshore. Their most exciting adventure involved the beaching on the shoals of the *Mariquita*, a twenty-seven-ton steam vessel carrying a Burlington baseball team returning home after a game. Chester rowed all of the passengers to the shore, where they proceeded to walk on the Rutland Railroad tracks to the mouth of the Winooski River. The *Mariquita* was pulled off the shoal the next day, only slightly the worse for the experience.

Arthur Lorenz, a single man from Germany, spent twenty-two years as keeper. For supplies, he would row four and a half miles to Port Kent or six and a half miles to Port Douglas once a week from April to December on a dory he had purchased himself. One time, heading into an east wind with the spray flying, he became coated with ice. Because his arms kept moving to row, he didn't notice that he had become encased in ice. He was frozen so stiff that upon his arrival at the lighthouse he couldn't get up. He had to chip away enough ice with his knife to get himself inside. Lorenz was one of the few who preferred staying at the lighthouse year-round. During one particular spring night, Lorenz heard a terrific roar and felt a jolt to the structure. Looking out, he saw nothing. His first reaction was fear that harm had befallen his beloved dory. Making his way downstairs, he was shocked to find the southwest corner of the kitchen being pushed in with the pressure of tons of ice. The grinding, splintering and smashing of ice continued. Then, just as quickly as it had begun, the wind shifted and "the pressure of the floes against the building relaxed and the pushed-up ice cakes slid back to lake level." But alas, he discovered that the precious dory he had bought with his own money was gone. The place was in shambles, but only one corner of the building had actually been smashed. While commiserating over his loss and the work ahead, he noticed a dark object on a large ice floe floating in the west. Could it be? Yes! His dory, bottom side up and apparently undamaged, was heading his way. He ran for his long pike pole and waited. When it was close enough, he snagged the ice cake, pulled it toward the reef and grasped his dory—in perfect condition! Lorenz recovered from the shock of being told to leave the lighthouse in

1931 because of his age (threescore and ten, or seventy years old), and he died before his plans to retire on a small farm in Jericho, Vermont, came to fruition.

The lighthouse was decommissioned in August 1933, when a blinker light was installed on one corner of the masonry foundation. After sixty-two years of service, the lighthouse was closed. In 1952, it was put up for sale by the U.S. Coast Guard. Fortunately, Manning notes, it came to "the attention of Mrs. J. Watson Webb who was then establishing the Shelburne Museum for the preservation of just such antiquities of the past." But would it be able to be moved given its construction of "the stoutest timbers and heaviest construction, securely anchored to its solid masonry foundation"?

Robert Francis shepherded the project that placed the lighthouse on a makeshift rig on August 1, 1952. Specific details of this historic and exciting move are contained in Manning's pamphlet, but suffice it to say that the move was a success. By the spring of 1953, the lighthouse had been returned to its original state and placed on the museum grounds.

Today, the Colchester Reef Lighthouse serves as "a museum within a museum." With oil and water paintings, colored lithographs depicting the ships of the day (clipper ships, whalers, paddle steamboats), and several heroic naval victories, the display also includes the austere furnishings of the keepers' rooms and reminds us of the "splendid isolation" of its inhabitants.

LIVING DAY TO DAY IN THE COLCHESTER LIGHTHOUSE

The Daily Log of Albert Hunter, 1898–1907

Anythin' for a quiet life, as the man said wen he took the sitivation at the lighthouse.
—Charles Dickens, Pickwick Papers 1836–1837

You will not find Albert Hunter's name on the list of lighthouse keepers. During the years of his daily recordings—from 1898 to 1907—the keepers noted are James Wakefield Jr. and Walter and, later, Chester Button. Albert was the farmhand/handyman who worked for many of the area's families, and one of his jobs for them was tending the lighthouse.

The recordings were discovered in the big red brick farmhouse on Holy Cross Road that formerly belonged to Lillian Ware. It had been the home of Henry Thayer. Thayer left the place to Ware, who had cared for him for many years until his death. Jean Morin found the recordings while cleaning out the attic following Ware's death. She lent them to Irving "Steck" Stecklare, whose relatives are frequently mentioned in the writings, and Joan Alden. They realized the significance of the journals and, working with Art Cohn of the Vermont Maritime Museum, had copies made that would be shared with the Burnham Memorial Library, the Colchester Historical Society, the museum and others. Their enthusiasm for what is now contained in two large, spiral-bound manuscripts is what will catch your attention.

Albert's handwriting was legible, although, depending on the writing instrument used, some pages scanned clearer than others. His language is simple yet profound when setting a scene or relating an experience. One recording leads to the next, and despite the size of the texts, reading on becomes irresistible. There are nine years of almost daily recordings. The following excerpts were selected to coincide with certain dates—Christmas, March Meeting Day, July 4, January 1, the last entry on May 24, 1907—and some just seemed interesting.

December 25, 1898
7 a.m. 30 degrees. Hardly any breeze. Noon—Still light but increasing SW, cloudy all over and equally all around. 12:15—Have been watching two loons on southwest side for past 10 minutes. They came up close twice, close together and not more than 4 rods out. Oh! How I wished I had a rifle. It looks as if we will have a breeze from the N before long. 12:40 27 degrees Wind shifted to N. And snow flying so I can hardly see Hog-back. 12:55 25 degrees—Both loons and gulls close by. 1:05 Oh! That loon not 100' away. He is a great aggravation to me. I wish I could catch him. Wind N Light. Swerving quite hard. 1:30 26 degrees—Snow storm over and sun shining. 3p.m. 25 degrees—Just through my Christmas dinner. I had potato, squash, turnip, cabbage, beets and stewed onions, wheat bread and donuts, tea and cold water butter and sweet pickles and if only Chet had been here to assist in stowing it away there would have been nothing lacking. However, it passed off very pleasantly but I don't feel now as if I should come to repeat it today.

January 1, 1899
12:01 3 degrees Wind N light. A Happy New Year to everyone.

April 24, 1899
8 p.m. After doing chores and eating breakfast, I started in my boat at 6:30 and reached here [the lighthouse] *at 8 p.m. There was no wind and has been none all day. I saw a pickerel about 15 inches long about 4 inches below surface of water with a lamprey eel hanging to him. I struck them with an oar before I remembered that I had a gun and could have shot them, and of course, I saw no more of them. About a dozen loons were within a mile of here and all laughing like fun. Because I had got back here I suppose. I shot at one at 6 p.m. but, of course, I missed. They have been around all day.*

May 10, 1899 [The next two notations refer to the Island Line railroad then under construction.]
It was quite sunny and I could see very well over to Grand Isle where the new railroad is being built. I could see the steam shovel work as well as hear it and also the pile driver. The evening fires are burning across the lake alongside of the railroad. They look quite cheerful and seem almost like company.

May 12, 1899
Can clearly see steam shovel work and cars dumping rocks that are loaded by shovel. Can also see the big red flatboat that went up yesterday p.m. loaded with lumber. The engine is still on board.

July 4, 1904
Wind from S so hard I dared not go ashore, so Chet went over to meet his company and celebrate on shore. A terrible S gale all day and into the night. Chet and his folks all went home to Colchester. He took the glass so I was alone really. A fishing fleet of 8 boats were off Barney Point most of the day.

August 30, 1906
Vacation Day—visited all day, first this summer. Called on Uncle Willard, and Mrs. Smalley and she showed me the new bathroom and water works, furnace, etc. Cook dinner at Will Coates and had very pleasant visit. Stopped at West Hinds. He and Henry dressing hog at 240—I guessed 237 ½. Stopped at Henry's and got 2 jars white vinegar and then went to Chet's and did chores. This evening carried Henry's crowbar home. Warm and pleasant.

November 16, 1906
Great snow storm. Biggest snow storm ever. All last night and all day. 18 and 20 inches on level. Two hours going from home to Chet and entry done up when I got there. Impossible to follow road for drifts. No mail and no road breaking. Staying overnight at Chet's.

May 24, 1907 [last entry]
Cold and warm. Pete Bessette finished plowing Chet's garden and planted 6 rows of Gold Coin potatoes in a.m. Made papering board and got ready to paper Chet's sitting room and found we hadn't enough so partly painted the room. Went over to Henry's this evening. Feel pretty tired and nearly used up.

Albert Hunter died alone a week later on May 31, 1907, at the age of sixty-three years. His mother was a Thayer and may be the reason he returned from Massachusetts at the age of fifty-four years.

Thanks to Joan Alden, Irving "Steck" Stecklare and David Coates for bringing this important discovery of Colchester history to the attention of the public.

Lighthouse Keepers

Herman Malaney, December 1, 1871 to October 16, 1882
Walter M. Button, December 11, 1882 to March 31, 1888
August Pare, June 27, 1888 to October 31, 1889
James Wakefield Jr., October 31, 1889 to July 7, 1890
Walter M. Button, July 7, 1890 to October 14, 1892
James Wakefield, October 14, 1892 to November 7, 1892
Walter M. Button, November 7, 1892 to April 15, 1901
Chester F. Button, April 16, 1901 to April 9, 1908
William H. Howard, April 8, 1908 to November 5, 1909
August Lorenz, November 5, 1909 to spring 1931
Joseph Aubin, spring 1931 to August 1933
Decommissioned in August 1933

CLAREY'S BAYSIDE

A Dream Vacation in Malletts Bay, Colchester

Contemplate this for just a moment: While living in a crowded city in New York, Massachusetts or Canada, you read about the "Bayside Resort on Malletts Bay in Vermont." There are housekeeping and non-housekeeping cabins and an eight-room lodge at reasonable rates from which to choose. There is plenty to do—a beach for swimming, rowboats and bicycles to rent, playground equipment and horseshoes, basketball or table tennis to play. There's even a caged monkey named Chico to watch. Ballgames can be played on a large field surrounded by the cottages, and there are fireplaces to gather around come evening.

Ah, but there's more than singing around the campfire for the tourists visiting Clarey's Bayside. Evenings in the Bayside Pavilion were a world of fun, offering a weekly schedule of skate and dance.

Monday: Ladies' Night
Tuesday : Club Night
Wednesday: Beginners' Night
Thursday: Ladies' Night
Friday: Fun Night

Saturday afternoon was reserved for the children to skate. Admission to skate was ten cents; the men paid forty cents for skates and the ladies only twenty-five. But what really drew the crowds were the Saturday night dances.

For almost forty years, between 1923 and 1963, the sights and sounds of the biggest and best traveling bands in the United States could be found on the corner of Lakeshore Drive and Blakely Road. What bands, you might ask? Does the Glenn Miller Band sound familiar?

"I remember the night the Glenn Miller band was here," says Ruth Morgan, granddaughter of owner George Clarey. "The cars were parked like they are now for the July Fourth Fair Day fireworks."

Ruth had to work that night, but she did manage to get Miller's autograph.

Other big names to spend an evening in Colchester were Louis Armstrong, Sammy Kaye, Benny Goodman, Guy Lombardo, Ozzie Nelson and his orchestra, Red Norvo and Mildred Bailey. Local bands such as Ernie Andrews, Joe Lechnyr, Bob Minotti and Burlington's Ray Dorey were featured as well, according to Albert Spaulding's *Colchester Chronicle* article of February 1, 1992.

Local resident Walter Munson, before he passed away, recalled Ernie Andrews:

> *He was one of my personal favorites and was a Saturday night regular for three seasons. The Bayside Pavilion brings back a lot of happy memories. I used to say, "I helped Clarey to pay his mortgage," that's how often I would go—Gosh, they had great bands there and I just loved to dance.*

Ruth says that in 1935 her grandfather enlarged the pavilion to accommodate three thousand dancers. According to Spaulding, the last band to play in the Bayside Pavilion was Ray Charles in 1963. In addition to the big bands, in 1937 Clarey brought Sally Rand, a well-known "Fan and Bubble Dancer" to Colchester. Before she was given permission to perform by the Liquor Control Board, "assurances had to be given that the gaping throng at the Lake Champlain resort would catch but fleeting glimpses of her form," the *Colchester Chronicle* of August 1996 notes.

Ruth Morgan recalls much from her youth and the summers spent at the Bayside. "My grandfather was frequently fined for possessing gambling devices," she says, "generally pinball machines and others referred to as 'one-armed bandits.'" She has a newspaper clipping that tells the story of Clarey being held up and shot. It seems that the burglars entered the building when Clarey was there. They had a gun. He had a gun. Unfortunately, their gun worked and his didn't. He was wounded in the leg, but the sight of his gun did scare them off.

The resort provided employment for a variety of residents—from carpenters, painters, plumbers and waitresses to housekeepers, office staff and cooks. Local businesspeople like Bill Fitzgerald, who owned a dairy, would deliver milk to the tourist cottages and to the restaurant. Charles "Pinky" Williams (after whom Williams Road is named) delivered the ice that was harvested right out of Malletts Bay in the winter and kept in specially insulated icehouses.

Clarey died at seventy-eight years of age, and his two daughters, Dorothy (Ruth's mother) and Marguerite "Peg," and their brother, Jimmy, took over the place. According to Dorothy Clarey Dunn, she supervised the staff, her sister took care of the office and "Jimmy handled the Pavilion." Their father had earlier sold the Dine and Dance Restaurant to two men named Harrington and DuBrul. The three children tried to buy it back but with

ROLLER SKATING
SUNDAY
AFTERNOON and EVENING
AFTERNOONS 25c, INCLUDING SKATES
GENTS 40c — EVENINGS 7:30 TO 11 P. M. — LADIES 25
SKATING EVERY NIGHT NEXT WEEK EXCEPT SAT.
JOIN BAYSIDE ROLLERWAY CLUB—NO CHARG
4-27-38
BAYSIDE PAVIL
Malletts Bay, Vt.
GRAND OPENIN
TUES., MAY
Swing and Sw
WITH THE 1938 MUSICAL
Sammy KAY
House
oors For
Season
TONIGHT
BAYSIDE
PAVILION
TEX ROSE
AND HIS
LONE STAR
RANCHERS
Featuring
Sally and
Smiling
BennyGoodma
Appears at Ba
This Evenin
Master of Swing Music W
Lead His Orchestra in On
Vermont Appearance
at Bayside
Dance-lovers in Burlington
vicinity will be tendered an
usual treat this evening w
"The Swing Master," Benny Go
man, and his famous radio and
ording orchestra make a pers
appearance at Bayside Pavil
Malletts Bay. This will be Go
man's first and only Vermont
pearance. Dancing will start
o'clock.

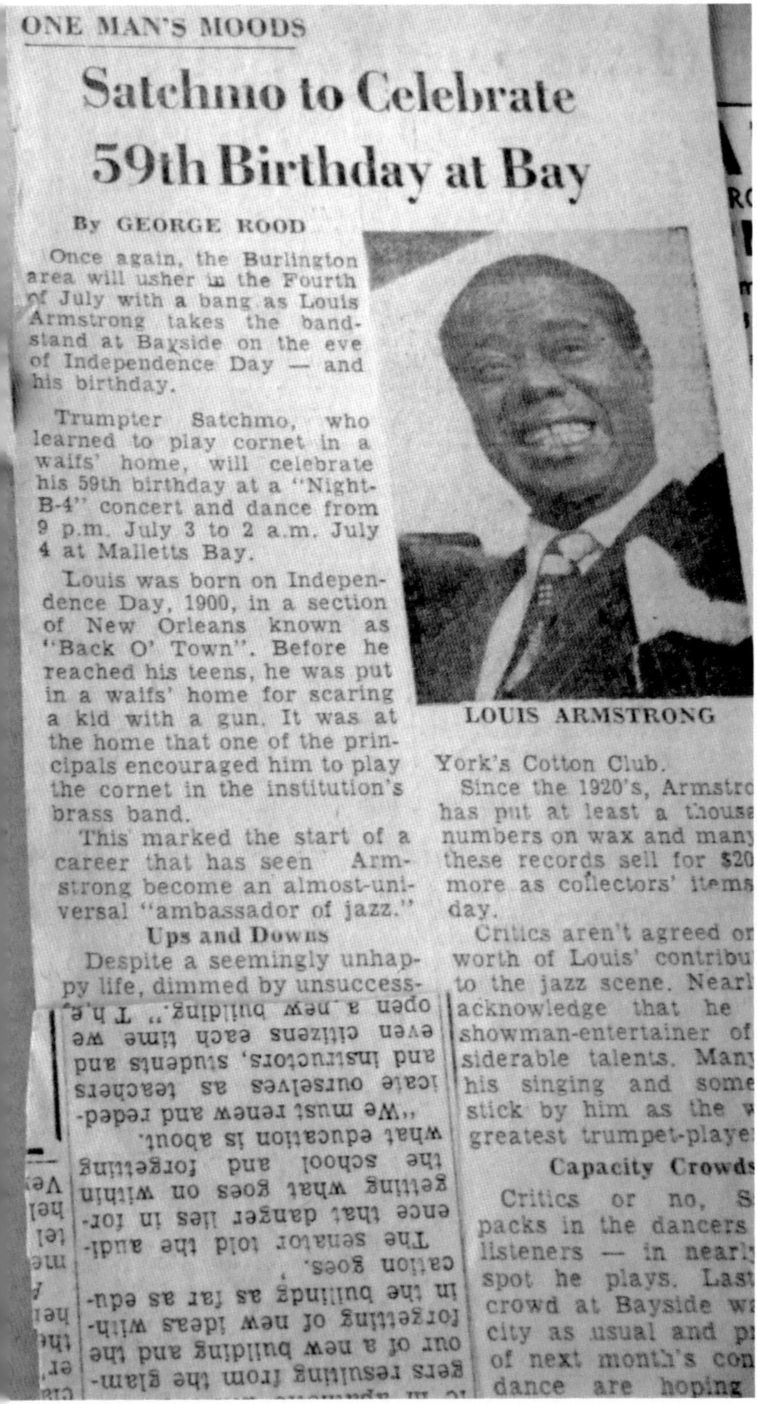

ONE MAN'S MOODS

Satchmo to Celebrate 59th Birthday at Bay

By GEORGE ROOD

Once again, the Burlington area will usher in the Fourth of July with a bang as Louis Armstrong takes the bandstand at Bayside on the eve of Independence Day — and his birthday.

Trumpter Satchmo, who learned to play cornet in a waifs' home, will celebrate his 59th birthday at a "Night-B-4" concert and dance from 9 p.m. July 3 to 2 a.m. July 4 at Malletts Bay.

Louis was born on Independence Day, 1900, in a section of New Orleans known as "Back O' Town". Before he reached his teens, he was put in a waifs' home for scaring a kid with a gun. It was at the home that one of the principals encouraged him to play the cornet in the institution's brass band.

This marked the start of a career that has seen Armstrong become an almost-universal "ambassador of jazz."

Ups and Downs

Despite a seemingly unhappy life, dimmed by unsuccess-

LOUIS ARMSTRONG

York's Cotton Club.

Since the 1920's, Armstro[ng] has put at least a thous[and] numbers on wax and many [of] these records sell for $20 [or] more as collectors' items [to]day.

Critics aren't agreed o[n the] worth of Louis' contribu[tion] to the jazz scene. Near[ly all] acknowledge that he [is a] showman-entertainer of [con]siderable talents. Many [like] his singing and some stick by him as the [world's] greatest trumpet-playe[r].

Capacity Crowds

Critics or no, S[atchmo] packs in the dancers [and] listeners — in nearl[y every] spot he plays. Last [year's] crowd at Bayside w[as ...] city as usual and p[...] of next month's con[cert and] dance are hoping

Advertisements heralding the arrival of "Big Bands" to Colchester. *Courtesy of Ruth Clarey Morgan.*

Ruth Clarey Morgan sits by her father's Bayside Pavilion, which offered a skating rink on weekdays and "Big Band" sounds every Saturday night. *Courtesy of Ruth Clarey Morgan.*

no luck. The restaurant changed under the new management, providing scantily clad girls dancing in full view of passing motorists. "My mother would call the police, but with no local police, it didn't help much," says Ruth. It wasn't long after that the pavilion was mysteriously destroyed by fire in 1964. Ruth says that the fire was traced to a wastepaper basket, and because propane gas tanks were involved, the firemen had no choice but to let the fire burn out.

The Bayside Pavilion, the Dine and Dance Restaurant and all of the memories they contained, were gone. For Ruth who had met her husband, Charles, on the skating rink, the evening of the fire was particularly painful. "We lived nearby and I walked to the fire, and I just couldn't believe it," she says.

Clarey's children decided shortly thereafter to sell the property to the town. "We didn't want high-rises to be built there," says Ruth. Her mother recalls that her father had also expressed his hope of selling the property to the town. Fortunately, as a member of the town's recreation board, Ruth was able to make the connection between the town and the family—"the deal was made with a promise and a handshake," she recalls. The total price for the twenty-five-acre lot with 540 feet of lakeshore was $150,000 in 1968. The cost to the town was only $37,500 because of Bureau of Outdoor Recreation (BOR) federal assistance. An auction of the cottages and all of the furnishings was held at the same time. A commemorative marker for George Clarey now rests on the beach side of the Bayside

A view of the Clarey's Resort cottages on Malletts Bay, Lake Champlain. *Courtesy of Greg Dirmaier.*

Park. The development of the park into the well-used recreation area we know today completes the story. And what a story it is!

Thanks to Ruth Morgan and Dorothy Clarey Dunn for the memories and for keeping them alive for all of us.

Nourse's Corner

It's funny what you remember years later about a job you had when you were fifteen years old. Gerry Sweeney, who is now deceased, remembered that he worked long days—from noon until eleven or twelve midnight, with an hour off for supper. He was paid ten dollars a week for six days of work "and was lucky to have the job," he recalled with a smile. The job was at Nourse's Hot Dog Stand.

George Nourse opened his hot dog stand (located at the curve at the intersection of Goodsell Point Road and Lakeshore Drive) in 1933. He began by selling pepper steaks and toasted hot dogs. According to Ruth Wright's *Colchester, Vermont: Ice-Cap to Interstate*, "in 1957 [Nourse] opened a 42' x 50'

Nourse's Corner, circa 1940s. *Courtesy of the Colchester Historical Society.*

modern restaurant over a free flowing spring." This building was later torn down and replaced with two condos that exist to this day.

The popular food stand, with its sloping sandy beach into Malletts Bay, provided hours of entertainment to folks who came from miles around to spend the day. Sweeney recalls the landing of a seaplane and a startup business offering boat rides, although, he said, "the boat never went over big." Nourse's also sponsored the Huskies Softball team—if you won the game, you'd get a hot dog and a soda—and a radio show in which "a guy would sing and do a little talking," remembered Sweeney. He added:

> *The Cavalry soldiers from Fort Ethan Allen would come down and with rakes and shovels; they would walk in the water up to their shoulders and would start raking into the beach. Everything they would rake up—clams, weeds, the like, they would then take away.*

The area was generally filled with summer cabin "colonies" that were rented by the week, month and season. Wright's book adds, "Evening summer traffic on VT 127 [Lakeshore Drive] became so heavy that deputy sheriffs were hired by the Selectmen to patrol it."

Local general storeowner Dick Mazza adds:

> *It was entirely different in those days—you could expect a whole new crowd of people coming in every week. They would come back year after year but the turnover was almost weekly. It's different now—most of those cabins are gone or converted to year-round homes.*

That may be the reason that Nourse's Restaurant, later called the Beachcomber, Captain Malletts and Gerard's, is no longer open for business.

The Poor Farm

According to *Vermont Saints & Sinners* by Lee Dana Goodman, "As early as 1779, the Vermont legislature had passed an act—still in effect—that each town was responsible for 'supporting and maintaining' its own poor." The Settlement Law of 1787, allowed towns to "warn out any transient person… who…in their opinion was likely to become chargeable to the town." Thus, folks who had not lived long in Colchester might be "removed" to their original town of residence. Ruth Wright notes:

> *Under law the town took care of the aged, orphaned and the mentally and physically unemployable. The support of the indigent, aged and orphaned was usually "bid off," the low bidder to furnish food, tobacco and nursing and the Selectmen medicines, bedding and clothing.*

Some agreements in the town treasurer's records include:

> *William Scott to keep Henry Shaddock to board and wash and mend his clothes and make his shirts for seventy-five cents per week…and keep his cow for the use of which he is to deduct four dollars and return the cow at the end of the year…1825; For supporting Frenchman when sick $12.60…1839; By order in favor of E. Wolcott Balance Due him for taking care of the Smith boy until 21 years old $20.00…1843.*

As to an actual "poor farm," Wright says that in 1843 Colchester turned down an article of warning that proposed "to buy a farm for the support of the poor." Later, in

> *1853, L.B. Platt, Charles Collins, William C. Whiteman and Thomas Brownell were appointed to "examine a suitable farm for the town poor" and in March of the next year the Town "voted to purchase a farm for the use of the poor on road No. 25 (to be known as Poor Farm Road)." On March 2, 1861, the selectmen signed a note to promise to "pay the town of Colchester $3,731 with interest…for the whole amount of purchase of Town farm and utensils."*

By 1916, substantial improvements had to be made to the town farm. Wright notes that "a veranda was built on the house and considerable work done on the cow barn at a cost of $3,500." Ten years later, a Dr. Thibault declared the house uninhabitable. However, in the next year, the overseer of the poor reported that the house "required one ton of pulp plaster to patch up the walls and ceilings" and declared it to be "free of vermin." As far as most folks can remember, the poor farm closed sometime in the 1940s. Poor Farm Road remains.

THE DAWN VALCOUR COMMUNITY/SHIPMAN HILL

In the 1970s, Colchester was home to a community espousing the philosophy of "absolute social freedom," whose only governing law was "complete, universal free love." No, this was not part of the Island Pond commune or a contemporary to Woodstock. This was in 1874, almost 150 years ago.

On September 11, 1874, the *Chicago Tribune* newspaper was quoted by the *Burlington Free Press* as follows:

> *Charmed with the views on community enterprise set forth by one Wilcox of Wisconsin, Orren Shipman, wealthy fool…has offered 200 acres of Valcour Island (in New York) and his homestead containing 210 acres (in Colchester, VT) to any community that will undertake to carry out Wilcox's ideas. The community has been formed and the property accepted.*

On August 27, a group of Wilcox's followers, twelve in all, left Chicago for the promised land. That land can be found on Malletts Bay Avenue by the Lavigne Road intersection. When word of this experiment spread, ten more "free lovers" arrived from the Midwest, and the Dawn Valcour Agricultural and Horticultural Association was incorporated under Vermont law. The commune didn't survive its first Vermont winter. During those months, Wilcox sold a deer owned by Shipman to pay off a community debt to a Burlington merchant. Shipman had Wilcox arrested, and on March 13, in a jury trial before William Kidder, Colchester justice of the peace, a verdict for the defendant was rendered. The following month, Mrs. Shipman denounced Wilcox in the local press as a "swindler, imposter and prince of braggers." The community broke up, and the "free lovers" scattered to parts unknown.

In November 1875, the *Burlington Free Press* announced that "free love in Vermont and the Dawn Valcour Community was busted and Shipman was sick." In June 1876, the farm was sold; Orren Shipman was dead by 1878. Shipman Hill remains, as does the land, which is still used for farming. Alas, free love—except in the wild—has left. Never a dull moment in Colchester… even then.

Champlain Airport

Kites Instead of Planes

Land on Colchester Point owned and farmed by the Porter family since the early 1800s provided a perfect landing strip for small planes in the 1940s. According to an article in *Look Around Colchester and Milton, Vermont*, prepared by the Chittenden County Historical Society, Charlie Brink bought from the Sand Dunes Corporation in 1945 the "place that offered level land, a barn that would serve as a hanger, and a house that left something to be desired." The deed also had the following restrictions attached to it: the "property was not to be used for a hotel, club, tenting or business purposes and shall not be subdivided for sale or otherwise, and that but one dwelling house shall be built thereon." No swine, poultry, goats or cattle were allowed on the property.

Brink had been flying since he was fourteen years of age, and he wanted to continue his hobby. He worked for Bell Aircraft at the time and had, at first, kept his plane at the Burlington Airport. Despite the deed's restrictions, the Champlain Flying Service came into being shortly after his purchase of the land. The privately owned airport leased out its hangars and offered fuel, air rides, maintenance and flying lessons.

The airport gained some notoriety in 1959 when one of the FBI's most wanted men, Frank Lawrence Sprenz, landed there during a snowstorm in a stolen plane. He asked Brink's wife, Virginia, for permission to leave his plane there, and she is said to remember him as "a rather nice young man." In the course of traveling back and forth to his girlfriend in Winooski, with the police at this point alerted and in hot pursuit, he managed to elude the authorities, despite hitting a pole at the corner of Prim and Route 127. He was not apprehended until sometime later.

When Brink suffered a heart attack in the 1980s limiting his ability to fly, he began looking for a buyer for the property. A large housing developer made an offer, but Vermont's Act 250 law, concerned about the wetlands and the neighboring Colchester Bog, and area residents' opposition to the project crushed the deal. The town of Colchester purchased the land in 1983 with Bureau of Outdoor Recreation (BOR) funds, which were matched by the state, for use as a recreational park. Colchester's recreation director, Betsy Terry Orselet, drew up a master plan for its use, and today Airport Park offers several baseball and soccer fields, tennis and basketball courts, a playground, a walking trail, a bathroom facility and a covered pavilion for picnics, along with a two-hundred-year-old schoolhouse that serves as a visitors' center and museum. Rather than planes flying overhead, on a clear day one can now see balls and kites instead.

THE CREAMERY

As far as early records show, William Johnson built the first Colchester creamery in the late 1800s. Thelma and Luther Heath, who bought the property on Main Street in 1956, did not realize until 1987 that this was the location of the first creamery. Coincidentally, Thelma's grandfather—Alonzo Wheeler—had been the creamery's manager in those early days. At the time of purchase by the Heaths, it was still being used as a creamery. "When we bought the place, it was filled with creamery equipment," remembered Thelma. "My mother-in-law took one look at it and said, 'You'll never make

Farmers bring their milk to a Colchester creamery, circa late 1800s. *Courtesy of Joyce Sweeney.*

a home out of this,' but," continued Thelma, "I said to myself, 'Oh, I think I can.'"

The Heaths converted the building into a warm, cozy home. Inside, there is no sign of the old creamery. Outdoors, however, the old well still stands, as does a huge cement enclosure that used to hold a water tank. Some of the barns were taken down, and the remaining one was "shortened" by Mr. Heath.

In the early days, farmers would bring their cans of milk to the creamery each morning to be separated into cream and skim milk. The skim milk was often sold back to the farmers to feed the hogs, and the cream went to make butter and cheese. In 1899, a group of Colchester farmers formed the Colchester Cooperative Butter and Cheese factory and leased the "spring rights" from Mr. Johnson. This creamery burned down about 1922, and that foundation can still (as of 1997) be seen behind the house. In 1927, a new creamery (the present house) was built. As more and more dairy production shifted to fluid milk, the creamery business faltered. It was eventually sold to the Milton Cooperative and was used only as a receiving station.

The Heaths have since passed away, and the property is now owned by Gardner & Gardner, which leases it. "Except for an enclosed porch, it looks pretty much the same as it did when the Heaths were here," says Charlotte Gardner. There are no remaining creameries in Colchester.

LANDMARKS II

Getting Better with Time

Law Island

The eight-and-a-half-acre island resting in the shallow water off Colchester Point adjoining the old railroad right of way (Causeway Park) was named for John Law, Esquire. He is described as "the eccentric individual who settled on the point, came from New London, Connecticut, was a man of liberal education, fine talents, but too liberal and high minded to be otherwise than poor," according to Burlington's *Historical Gazette* in 1868. Law lived in the Colchester Point area with John M. Lane, and according to *Hemingway's Vermont Gazetteer*, he bought the farm "and what is now called Law's Island where he made an improvement, planted corn, raised wheat, potatoes, etc." In 1793, he was sent as the town delegate to the state convention at Windsor to consider the proposed amendments to the constitution. He served as a town representative to the legislature from 1801 to 1802 and was a second judge of Chittenden County Court for six years. Interestingly, local resident David Coates recalls his grandfather referring to the island as "Ben Law's Island," but there is no further reference found to explain the different first name.

Law Island was mentioned in a civil suit in 1803, when S. Campbell of Grand Isle sued S. Houston of South Hero for defamation of character. It appears that Houston had said in public that Campbell, in addition to other crimes, was a pumpkin thief and stole potatoes from Law Island. Campbell won and received $243 in damages and costs.

Donald Fuller, a member of the area's Porter family, says that after Bernard Homer Porter acquired the island, seven members who formed a club subsequently owned it. These included Ed Watkins, Hiram Merrihew and others. They built a clubhouse on the high part of the west side of the island, but it burned down before 1920. According to Fuller, Watkins so dominated the club that the others sold out their shares to him. Watkins's sons—Claude, who started the Sunset Drive-In in 1948, and Ira—later owned the island. Ira lost his share of the island to Claude and went on to Florida, where he had a circus animal act. He was known to bring his chimpanzees to the island. During the 1930s and 1940s, Claude summered on the island, and he and others were known to drive their cars through the shallow waters in late summer to get to the island (that roadway is no longer useable). When Claude sold the drive-in, he also sold the island, and there have been a string of owners since then. In 1994, the island was purchased by the Lake Champlain Land Trust (LCLT) for $229,900 and placed in perpetual conservation easement. Simultaneously, the LCLT transferred ownership of the island to the Vermont Department of Forests, Parks and Recreation, with Colchester and the Colchester Land Trust agreeing to serve as caretakers.

The future of Law Island and its care continues to rest with the state, with the Lake Champlain Committee and Colchester's Recreation and Parks Department serving as managers. Department director Glen Cuttitta says:

> *The Island is one of the stops on the Lake Champlain Committee's "Paddlers Highway," so the Lake Champlain Committee has taken an active stewardship role for the island and have been working to remove the dilapidated buildings. The Army Corps of Engineers may help with the project to assure those buildings are removed in an environmentally safe way.*

For those who have never been on the Causeway Park bike path or paddled by Law Island in their canoe or kayak, now is the time. It is a beautiful small island with majestic views—so come on down!

The Island Line...Was a Mighty Fine Line

More than one hundred years ago, specifically on January 7, 1901, the Rutland Island Line began service from Burlington to Alburgh. (Please note that on its first train schedule the small island community was, indeed, spelled with the *h*, just as it is today, although for many years in between, one would read Alburg, without the *h*.) That run took almost two hours from the city's Union Station to Alburgh, where it continued on to Montreal, Quebec, ending in Sorel, Canada. The train did not stop in Colchester but left its mark on the community with its rails that now constitute Causeway Park, a bike and walking path offering some of the state's most breathtaking views of Vermont's Green Mountains and Lake Champlain.

The three-and-a-quarter-mile causeway of riprapped marble across Malletts Bay connecting Colchester and South Hero and continuing to Alburgh was completed in just a year, beginning in 1899. The rail bed from Colchester Point to Allen's Point at South Hero cost the Rutland Railroad in the vicinity of one million dollars. Some of that money was raised from Dr. William Seward Webb and the New York Central Railroad owned by the Vanderbilt family.

The Island Line built in 1900 by the Rutland Railroad connecting Vermont to Canada. It ran until 1963. Today, the Causeway Park is used as a biking and walking path. *Courtesy of Local Motion Trails and Bikeways.*

When construction began in 1899, five hundred men, many of them Italian immigrants living in the Barre, Vermont area, were brought in as laborers. Locals also found employment and earned money by providing room and board to the imported laborers. Equipment, such as steel rails, plates and ties, was moved over the ice from Plattsburgh. "Steam drills, hoisting machines, and boiler dump cars were also drawn over this way," a Rutland Railroad log recorded.

The small bridge by Law Island in Colchester used a 96-foot steel girder, but little else is known of this smaller connecting bridge. The abutments for the 196-foot drawbridge before Allen Point on the tip of South Hero are still in place on both sides of the "cut" in the causeway that opens Malletts Bay to the broad part of Lake Champlain. The maximum depth of the cut at low water can be less than 9 feet between the two points and is the only opening between Malletts Bay and the lake. On the Rutland Railroad website (home.att.net/~rutlandrr/story/.html), Steve Mumley recalls:

> *I remember going to Burlington with my mother on the train (called the Green Mountain Flyer), and waving to the people in the little cottages. These were the living quarters for the people that manned the draws. The draws would only be open during navigation season, and I believe three or four people would be stationed at each of the three locations (the other two were on the Islands)…the draws were manually opened and closed. I don't believe they even had electricity out to the draws. I know they used kerosene lamps for light.*

He also recalls the signal light out on the fill that was operated by a storage battery stored in a cement box in the ground:

> *The batteries lasted a long time because the signal was only on when the draw was opened and turned on by the draw tender…I believe the Allen Point's draw had a newer search beam type signal. These signals were called approach and were "x" number of feet from the draw to prevent the trains from going into the drink.*

The three drawbridges were designed by Charles F. Stowell of Albany, New York, and were built of open-hearth steel. Because of their infrequent use, the draws were designed to be operated by hand.

> *The devices for working the signals, latches, end supports, turntable, all interlocked so they could only be moved in proper*

The Island Line roars across the marble rail bed from South Hero to Colchester. *Courtesy of Local Motion Trails and Bikeways.*

> *sequence. When the draw was closed, the only machinery that could be moved was the signal apparatus that operated home and distant signals at both ends of the bridge. When this was thrown to "danger" the latch lever was released and the latches could be drawn, unlocking the end supports* [rollers]. *Not until this was done was it possible to swing the bridge 180 degrees.*

George Sorrell, who served as draw tender for the Bow Arrow Bridge on the Islands, recalls:

> *We lived in a three-room house, two bedrooms and a kitchen. It was single boarded, and when it came fall and high winds, you'd freeze to death… The first thing you had to do was unlock the bridge; it was all interlocked electrically, run by batteries. Then you put your signals on. Almost a mile either side of the bridge if a train came along and hit this one piece of track it put the lights on, a green over red. But if he got two reds right above the other, he'd know the bridge was open and he'd cut his speed down so that when he got to the "home signal," which is 300 feet from the bridge, he'd stop there and stay there until we got the bridge closed and locked and we'd throw the levers and he'd get a green signal. Then there was the train going by three feet from your bedroom window. Your dishes would rattle. After awhile we wouldn't hear it but you'd always hear a boat when it came…You started on the bridge the first of May and most generally got done the first of December, or whatever date the navigation closed…We ate a lot of fish and frog legs.*

The largest of the swinging drawbridges built by the Rutland Railroad on the 3.4-mile causeway connecting Colchester to South Hero. It cost $1 million and employed five hundred men. *Courtesy of Local Motion Trails and Bikeways.*

During World War I, both the Rutland and Central Railroads were taken over by the federal government. In 1919, in disrepair, the railroad was returned to the Rutland Railroad. It struggled along until 1961, when the strikebound Rutland, its passenger and milk traffic a fading memory, called it quits. In 1963, Vermont appropriated $2.7 million to acquire the Rutland tracks within the state.

Brian Costello of Local Motion, an organization that promotes national rail to trail development, says that they hope to eventually replicate the draw tender as a rest area at the "cut."

Having learned about the Island Line that ran through Colchester connecting Rutland and Burlington to Canada, it may be of interest to know if the railroad ever stopped here. A small flag station was built in the Mills and Colchester Point area. The only "station agent and telegraph-operator on duty for long hours," however, was not found in the "Point" area of town; instead, he was located off East Road in the village. According to Ruth Wright's *Colchester, Vermont: Ice-Cap to Interstate*, commissioners of the railroad met in November 1849 at Ward's Hotel in Milton to award damages to residents of northeastern Colchester over whose land the six-rod railroad, running from northwestern Vermont to Painesville, crossed. The latter, completed early in 1851, provided permanent jobs for a dozen persons at the Colchester depot and on the track section. It appears from Wright's notes that the Central Vermont Railroad closed this depot in the early 1940s. There are today no visible remains of the Colchester depot. Only the name, Depot Road, remains on the road sign.

MALLETTS HEAD

Ties Colchester to the Nation

Malletts Head, on the west side of the inner bay separating the inner from the outer bay of Lake Champlain, is rumored to have been Captain Mallett's home. It is somewhat isolated so was fitting for the man many suggest was a hermit.

According to *Look at Colchester and Milton, Vermont*, from the Chittenden County Historical Society, "In 1854, Bartholomew Reagen (also spelled Regan and Ragan) owned three farms and a large orchard on the headland called Malletts Head." According to *Child's Business Directory of 1882*, there were four Reagans—David, Bartholomew, Daniel and Michael. *Beer's 1869 Atlas of Chittenden County* shows three Reagans owning land that they farmed on Malletts Headland (off Marble Island Road). One other name, the Winooski Marble Company, was also listed as an occupier of this large acreage. According to *Colchester, Vermont, Ice-Cap to Interstate*, in the 1850s David Read became enthusiastic over the possibilities of commercial use of the dolomite rock on the headlands. He and a group of promoters, including George Marsh, a Mr. Freeman and Henry Keyes, acquired all rocks, stones and quarries on the headland, Marble Island, Newton's Point (later called Coates Island) and the ledges east of Bean Road. They cut three roads—one parallel with Prim Road, another to Newton's Point and one to Marble Island. The marble was red in color or a shaded green—all was beautiful, albeit brittle and hard. One of the quarries was so accessible that a vessel could be brought up alongside and loaded with ease. Some of the marble from Colchester was used in the national Capitol and the Albany capitol buildings. The marble business was not profitable, however, and Hazen and Lyon Quarry finally sold the contents of the marble mill at auction. The buildings were converted to recreational use.

According to the Chittenden County Historical Society book:

> *The old mill was referred to as "Mrs. Ricker's resort"* [Mrs. Ricker was the widow of Gustav, one of the operators of the mill] *when it was sold to T. Russell "Rusty" Brown of New York in 1919. He was given a 5-year tax exemption by the town and set about improving the docking facilities and installing a 9-hole golf course.*

He constructed an indoor skating rink over the beautiful marble floors of the Marble Island building, which burned down in 1996. He also built a six-hundred-foot toboggan chute where boats are now stored. According to Dawn Hazelett, this was a little dangerous, "so it was later moved to the left of the clubhouse, just about at the bend in the road." Brown met an untimely death in 1939, when a water tank exploded. According to Hazelett, after Brown's death, Winthrop Coffin owned it until his death, at which time daughter Barbara Coffrin Jones took over. The family still owns Rose and Cave Islands and the Three Island Sailing Yacht Club (the third island in the cluster is Marble Island, which has since reverted to the protection of the State of Vermont). In 2009, on the old Marble Island Resort property, private homes are now being constructed. A public marina exists as well.

The other half of the headland was sold at the turn of the century to John George MacVicar of Montclair, New Jersey, who assembled a family organization that included his wife's sister, her husband and his brother (the Ames family). According to John Ames, MacVicar's nephew:

> *He always wanted to run a boys camp so first acquired the lease on a non-operating marble mill and founded the Champlain Camp* [its early seasons were run on what is now the Marble Island Resort]. *He then purchased from the Reagans what is today the Brown Ledge Camp and moved the operation over there* [the camp was purchased by the Browns in 1926 and is now a girls camp].

The now private residential area (Malletts Bay Club Road) is home to "handsome structures that must be of a quality approved by the corporate owner selling the site," the Chittenden County Historical Society book notes. One more island in the group rests just off Brown Ledge Camp and is called Hazen or Camp Island, and another just off the Marble Island Club Road complex is Birch Island. Interestingly, these last two islands are remembered by area resident David Coates as being called King's Island and Queen's Island. These islands add diversity and interest to Malletts Bay, and together with the tales of a hermit's home, the existence of colorful and exotic stones and the early settling families, they provide even more spice to this part of Colchester.

A History of the Burnham Memorial Library

Written and researched by Maureen Dakin and Carolyn Barnes in 1997

Books are gates to lands of pleasure,
Books are keys to wisdom's treasure,
Books are paths that upward lead,
Books are friends—Come let us read.
—Poem from the Burnham Memorial Library dedication ceremonies, August 14, 1942.

When "Let's go to the Library" is heard around town, it generally means going to the public library located on the green at 898 Main Street in the village. Not many say "Let's go to the Burnham Memorial Library," and yet the Burnhams were real live people with a strong community spirit and a desire to use their good fortune to benefit the town for generations to come.

The library is named for Herbert and Electa Burnham because Electa (Etta) Burnham left most of her estate to build a library in memory of her husband and to establish a trust to maintain it. Their painting hangs over the fireplace, and their gravestone is in the cemetery just behind the library.

Mrs. Burnham was born in Colchester in 1863, the daughter of Francis Cook and Eliza Day Cook, and grew up on a farm on Mill Pond Road. Herbert, a third-generation Vermonter, was born in Johnson, Vermont, in 1859. Etta and Herbert Burnham were married in Colchester in 1883 and moved to Gardner, Massachusetts, where he was vice-president of the American Oil Stove Company. The Burnhams were active in church and community in Gardner, particularly in youth work. The couple had no children.

After Mr. Burnham's retirement in 1926, the couple returned to Colchester and settled quickly into small-town life. He held several town offices and was active in the Grange. She was a member of the King's Daughters at the Congregational Church and was chair of the library trustees. Herbert died in 1932 on a trip to California. Mrs. Burnham continued living in Colchester and remained active in the community until her death in 1939. In her will, she left most of her estate to build, furnish and maintain a library. Her stated preference was for a building similar to the one in Underhill Flats to be built on Church Park. Her wish for the location was honored when the land was leased from the church for one dollar. The land was not purchased by the town until plans for the addition were underway.

The building was designed by Newton and Rhodes and was built by Roux of Springfield, Massachusetts, for a total cost of $4,650, including paneling and shelving. Groundbreaking was in August 1941, and the library was dedicated on August 14, 1942.

At the time the new Burnham Memorial Library opened, the population of the town was 3,031. Colchester Village was surrounded with working farms, and it was a real center of activity, with a creamery, churches, stores, gas stations, a town clerk's office and a post office. In its first year in the new building, the library had 2,258 books, circulation was 3,562 and the total library budget was $229.76. The library was open on Wednesday afternoons and evenings. Children's and adults' books were all on the main floor, with a small table and chairs in the children's corner.

The Burnham Library was not the first library in town. It had its beginnings as the King's Daughters' Library. The King's Daughters is a women's group of the Congregational Church that performs charitable and service functions, as well as being a social and devotional group. The minutes of the September 7, 1900 meeting of the King's Daughters note, "It was voted to use at least a part of our funds in the coming year in starting a Public Library." At that time, the group had twenty-five members with familiar Colchester names such as Munson, Severance, Collins and Wright. Through fundraising efforts such as a Maple Sugar Social, Lawn Party and Suppers for group members (ten cents a supper), the group had fifty dollars in the bank by February 1901 for the library fund—not a trifling amount for a small group to raise in just five months at the turn of the century.

The library opened on September 1, 1901, in rooms over Wolcott's store (corner of East Road and Main Street), rented for $4.00 a month. The King's Daughters paid $1.50 per month for the rent, the remainder being paid to Miss Hill and Miss Crockett, who were to live there, with Miss Hill acting as librarian. On opening day, there were forty-seven books on the shelves, purchased for a total of $35.00. For the next ten years, the library was run by a committee, with members appointed quarterly. A birthday party for the library each September provided much of the income for book purchases and operating expenses.

The library changed location several times in its first few years. In 1908, it was moved to Mrs. Amelia MacNeil's house, right across the street from the present library, and remained there for more than thirty years.

In 1911, the King's Daughters Circle voted to turn the library over to the town. The town meeting appropriated fifty dollars for the operation of a library, the first slate of five trustees was elected and the library was renamed the Colchester Free Library. The town appropriation for the library remained fifty dollars throughout the 1920s and 1930s, twenty-five dollars a year for Mrs. MacNeil and the balance for books. The library was open just about any time Mrs. MacNeil was home, essentially seven days a week. She checked out about fifteen hundred books a year (about what is checked out in a week today), not including children's books placed in the one-room schoolhouses. After Mrs. MacNeil's death, the library moved to the "brick building" where Village Cutters is now and stayed there until 1942, when the books were moved to the new Burnham building on Church Park.

The Burnham Memorial Library. *Photo by Hank Schaefer.*

The building remained much the same from 1942 to 1989, while the collection grew, programs evolved and use of the library increased. Joyce Sweeney remembers coming with her school class to the library to check out books. Hester Sweeney, librarian from 1960 to 1988, remembers these lunchtime visits from the librarian's point of view: "It was fun but hectic with twenty or thirty children choosing and signing out books in a short time." In snowy weather, the brown linoleum was awash in salty water by the time the classes left, and Hester had no choice but to get out the mop. Hester used her own portable Royal until the library acquired a typewriter, and she said she urged the trustees for years to install a telephone. Trustees of earlier years felt strongly that the library should be used only for library purposes. Longtime trustees were distressed when new trustees in the 1970s wanted to use the building for other purposes. But, Hester said, they were wonderful years, and she wouldn't have traded them for anything.

Highlights from this period include:

1952: Card catalogue ready for use, after two years of volunteer effort.
1960: Hester Sweeney hired as librarian.
1967: Typewriter purchased.
1972: Telephone arrived.

1974: Trustees received federal grant to improve library facilities; downstairs remodeled for meeting rooms.
1977: Book Drop at Chittenden Bank established.
1979: Photocopier purchased and downstairs redecorated as a children's room.
1988: Friends of the Library formed.

By the 1980s, the library was "bulging at the seams," with books crammed onto extra shelves and lined up on the floor. A major addition was completed in June 1989, quadrupling the size of the library. The addition was designed by Michael Dugan, built by Wright and Morrissey and funded by a bond and $100,000 from Library Services and a Construction Act grant. In the seven years since the addition was completed, annual circulation has tripled to more than seventy thousand. The book collection has doubled in size; books on tape, videotapes, music on tape and CDs have their place in the library, too. A computer donated by IBM, Inc. in 1989 allowed the library to connect to VALS (Vermont Automated Library System); that same year, the library converted to a fully automated circulation system (no more hand-stamping books).

Computer use has become a mainstay of the library's services. There are now thirteen computers for public use in the library: five for adults, four for children, two for teens and two laptops for use in the library. In 2000, the library purchased a used step-van for use as a summer bookmobile, and by 2003, the library had purchased a custom-built bookmobile (funded by a national grant from the Institute of Museum and Library Services), which provided service to neighborhoods farther away from the library. The library sold the bookmobile in 2007 and currently provides outreach to day cares, senior centers and individuals through weekly visits by library staff.

In 2007–08, the Friends of the Burnham Library raised more than $20,000 in its first public fundraising campaign, allowing the Burnham Library to provide music programs, local history talks, a meet-the-author series, additions to the endowment, music purchases, summer reading programs for both teens and children and a day-long festival of world music that celebrated the diverse backgrounds of families living in Colchester. The library continues to host programs for all ages and also provides a public meeting space for community groups to hold meetings at the facility.

Trustees noted in their minutes: "[Mrs. Burnham] caught a vision, dreamed a dream, and laid foundation sure. She prayed, she planned, she worked and wrought to make a dream endure." The library building that Mrs. Burnham envisioned certainly has endured, and wouldn't she be pleased to see how bright and busy it is now!

Information for this article was derived from the Minutes of the Opportunity Circle of the King's Daughters, *from the minutes of the Board of Trustees, and from research done by Barbara Wicker on Mr. and Mrs. Burnham. At the first writing of this article in February 1997, Carolyn Barnes was librarian of the Burnham Memorial Library and Maureen Dakin was BUCK chairperson for the Friends of the Library. Ginger Gellman, publicity and adult programming assistant, updated the article in 2009.*

SCHOOLING

The Old Fashioned Way

The first constitution of Vermont (1777) stated that a school or schools must be provided in every town, and a tax for said provision was to be assessed, according to Ruth Wright's book, *Colchester, Vermont, Ice-Cap to Interstate*. Thus, in 1794, a meeting was called to vote on dividing the town into districts "for the benefit of schools." In 1801, the town was divided into four districts that would be designated by a number. District No. 1 would include the Pine Island area of the Intervale running north to Colchester Bay. District No. 2 extended to the Essex line from the southeast corner of town and "intersects with the southwesterly district—southerly to Onion River" and was to be considered the southeasterly district.

> *District No. 3 beginning at the southwesterly corner of lot No. 50…where Simeon Hine now lives…and thence running south 54 degrees east on the Town line between Colchester and Milton to the corner of Sd Towns and thence south 36 degrees west on the line between Colchester and Essex…it being the North East District in said Town.*

District No. 4 became known as the northwest district.

It is difficult to accurately determine what school building belonged to what district, but a later district, No. 5, which was also called the southwest

Colchester Center School on Main Street. The land was donated by William B. Munson, who had fourteen children. It also served as a religious and civic meetinghouse and town hall. The two-story brick building still stands today. *Courtesy of the Colchester Historical Society.*

district, is clearly identified as the Colchester Point School or the Porters Point School, as it is known today.

According to Wright's book, "early school buildings were usually cheap structures, probably plank-sided and ortise-silled and never adequately repaired." The land was usually the most worthless in the area, often exposed to sun and winter wind. "Interiors were unlined and unplastered, poorly ventilated and cold in winter." Furnishings were sparse—a fireplace, "a slant-desk nailed to one or more sides of the room with a shelf beneath for caps, mittens and dinner buckets; a double row of benches on three sides of the room, an elevated platform for the teacher's desk" and an assortment of paper, ink ("made from the inner bark of the red maple"), quill pens and books. School sessions revolved around farming schedules. Boarding of the teacher was often bid off (the lowest bidder got the teacher), and families were expected to "furnish wood, cut and piled near the schoolhouse door by mid-December" (or pay extra). While "English reading, writing and arithmetic" were to be taught based on 1797 law, by the mid-1800s, Wright notes, "orthography, reading, writing, English grammar, geography, arithmetic, history of the United States, and good behavior" were added as required subjects.

The 1806 school census listed twenty-two "scholars" in the southwest district; in the 1833 census, that district, or District No. 5, had forty-six

The McBride School on East Road was built of brick. It was later used as a loom room but deteriorated and is no longer in existence. *Courtesy of the Colchester Historical Society.*

pupils attending school for thirty-two weeks. In 1845, Wright notes, sixty-five students attended for "3 of the winter months and 4 mos of 'sumer' school." In 1867, state law required children between eight and fourteen years of age to attend public schools at least three months a year; in 1870, a minimum of twenty weeks of school a year was made mandatory. In 1908, the law changed to a mandatory sixteen years, or until a child passed the ninth grade. From the 1864 town report, we have the following summary for District No. 5:

> *Teachers wages w/board: $147.00; fuel and misc.: $27.69; repair on buildings: $2.10; 28 weeks of school; avg. wages paid: $5.25 a week; 67 students with $141.75 listed on the Grand List.*

There were eighty-seven students in 1877 at a cost to the district of $83.03. The total school budget in that year was $1,161.82, with fourteen school districts (or individual school buildings).

In 1873, Superintendent Ballard said of the Colchester Point School: "60 different 'schollars' of all ages are packed in a room that would suitably accommodate 35 or 40." In 1884, Superintendent O.W. Peck was very glad to report that District No. 5 had "replaced the old style straight backed benches which cause round shoulders, flat chests and deformed spines, with properly folded chairs of a smart and approved pattern." According to Wright, in the early 1900s, "three or four children were crowded into the double seats at the old one-room brick Colchester Point School where one teacher, Muriel Douglas, was valiantly instructing 42 pupils in the eight grades." In 1926, the "new Point school building with coat rooms and inside chemical toilets, won a Proctor prize of $100 as a superior school." In the 1930s school PTAs (Parent-Teacher Associations) were formed. "The PTA backed the hot lunch program, mothers alternating in working at the school during the preparation, serving and cleaning up after a hot noon meal." Helen Paquette remembered those days, saying, "We used to alternate making the hot soup in our own kitchens to bring to school to go with their sandwiches."

A Union high school committee in 1950–51 diligently studied a possible regional high school for Colchester, Jericho, Richmond, Williston and Underhill. In 1951, in a 147–136 vote, two buildings financed by a $117,000.00 bond issue resulted in one school in the village (Union Memorial School), and the other at Colchester Point (across from the old Colchester Point School). In 1951, the legislature set a school year at 170 days, and Colchester received $20,522.79 in state aid for its 384 children of school age. The school tax rate was $4.20, and the 1951 census showed the town to be the twentieth most populous of the school systems in the state. In 1975, a high school, located on Blakely Road, was finally opened.

In year 2009, the town of Colchester has one high school, a middle school and three elementary schools that serve a population of 2,212 students.

THE LAMENTATIONS OF AN 1869 SCHOOL SUPERINTENDENT

The following comments were excerpted from an annual report prepared by L.H. Elliot, superintendent of schools (Colchester), dated February 15, 1869. Some of his comments are amusing, while others are prophetic. All are interesting.

> *Most of the schools have been under the care of efficient teachers, but a few have been nearly worthless, simply because the districts were determined to have* cheap *teachers. It seems to me that, if some districts would change their policy, and secure well-tried and efficient teachers, without regard to cost, their schools would be greatly improved.*
>
> *So many things combine to make a good school, such as a good teacher, interested parents, a suitable schoolhouse, desirable apparatus, etc., that your Superintendent does not feel justified in naming any one teacher as the best. And, if he did, his decision, based upon one or two visits, might be very incorrect. He does feel safe, however, in saying no school in town is so far advanced that it cannot be greatly improved. Neither is any school so backward that it should be given up as hopeless.*

Here Superintendent Elliot speaks about the condition of the school buildings:

> *As long as these unsightly and uncomfortable buildings remain unchanged, no parent can reasonably expect his children will love to go to school or will make rapid progress. He may expect that they will acquire great dislike for education…I would suggest to every district the desirableness of covering the dingy walls of their school room with a coat of paint or white-wash…I am glad to make an exception of the one in district No. 7. The citizens of that district deserve great credit for the improvement they have made in their school building…Will not other districts follow this example?*

On the subject of resources, Superintendent Elliot wrote:

> *With the exception of district No. 14, every school house has a black-board, or an apology for one; but many of them are so small or so poor that they are nearly useless…Not a school house in town has a map of Vermont…No house has that almost indispensable assistant in the successful study of Geography, a globe…As for dictionaries…not one can be found. These few articles could be purchased for less than thirty dollars, while no money invested would bring so large returns.*
>
> *Your attention is called to the fact that many children in town do not attend school…Where are the remaining children? And where is our school law, compelling parents to send their children to school three months a year?*
>
> *Greater interest ought to be manifested in the work done in the school-room. It is a lamentable fact that, in some districts, none of its citizens have*

entered the schoolhouse during the year; in others, only one or two, and in no district, does the register show the names of one-twentieth of the citizens.

I wish further to ask the committees in the several districts to request the teachers to appear at the public examination. Only seven of the twenty-five teachers in town, this year, were publicly examined. The citizens, too, should come and see how the teachers stand the test. I would also suggest that the several districts should withhold from their teachers all pay for services performed previous to the time of their examination.

If the citizens of Colchester will act upon these several suggestions, regard to better teachers, better school-houses, a supply of needful apparatus, and an increased interest in the work done in the school-room, and in the many children who neglect school, I am confident that the cause of Education will be greatly advanced.

SUMMER CAMPS

IN THE GOOD OLD SUMMER TIME

Because of the enormous amount of Lake Champlain shoreline in Colchester, several summer camps have been part of its culture for years. Few are left in 2009, so it becomes even more important to remember their history, purpose and impact on the town of Colchester.

Starting with the oldest, Brown Ledge Camp originally began as the Champlain Camp for boys and was started by the MacVicars family in 1897. According to Bill Neilsen, camp director when this article ran in the *Colchester News Magazine* in 1996, the camp leased the land from the Malletts Bay Club and operated for eight or nine years. It lay unused for about fifteen years until Harry E. and Marjorie P. Brown bought it in 1926. Bill said that the "difference" for this camp today is the same as it was when the Browns and, later, their daughter Barbara Winslow ran the camp. According to Bill:

> *That "difference" stems from the two approaches used by the camp. As far as the activities program goes, the female campers attend what they want, when they want, with whom they wish, for as long as they wish. For instance, if they only want to sail for the four or eight weeks, they can do that. However, usually they try a bit of everything before they decide on what to concentrate. The other difference is in their living quarters. Four to five girls stay in a cabin together. They can decorate it*

Champlain Camp for boys started in 1897. It later became the Brown Ledge Camp for girls. *Courtesy of the David Coates family and Greg Dirmaier.*

the way they want, etc. Their counselor lives close by but separately, and is readily available should they need her. We enable the girls to make their own decisions, to live independently—they have the opportunity for self-discovery and self-realization.

When Winslow decided to retire in 1983, she convinced a group of camp alumni to buy it. The 150-plus owners hired the Neilsens to run the camp, located on Malletts Bay off Marble Island Road, and they have continued as its directors until now. The camp's program is strong in horsemanship, with forty-three horses on site, as well as theatre (drama and stagecraft) and waterfront activities. Tennis, archery, riflery, arts and crafts, field trips and special events fill out the program list. Over the summer, approximately 180 campers will come from the United States, Canada, Mexico, South America and Europe. Counselors are from the United States, Europe and Australia. In 2009, for the eight-week session, the cost is $6,600, and for four weeks, $4,600. The camp is accredited by the American Camp Association.

On the shores of the Great Back Bay of Lake Champlain facing the Adirondacks lies Camp Kiniya. Its 150 acres, with one mile of waterfront, are nestled where the Lamoille River empties into the lake, at the very end of Camp Kiniya Road in the Clay Point area of Colchester. It was Helen Van Buren who named the camp *Kiniya*, an Indian word meaning "renewal of the spirit." It doesn't take but one look across the pine woods, open fields and sandy beaches with a magnificent view of the mountains and lake to understand why she chose Kiniya.

Helen Van Buren was a piano teacher in Burlington. During the summers, she would stay in Malletts Bay and would often canoe past the Clay Point property. In 1919, she finally bought it. She opened the girls' summer camp in 1920 with an emphasis on music and outdoor life; it remained in her hands for twenty-six years. Harry and Marjorie Brown, who also ran Brown Ledge Camp, owned it for the next six years, until Marilyn and Jack Williams bought it in 1951. "I had been a counselor at Brown Ledge Camp," said Marilyn when interviewed in May 1996.

"When the Browns had a reunion of camp counselors, they asked us if we'd be interested in buying the property," she added. Jack, who was working for the American Red Cross Aquatic Program at the time, had seen a lot of camps and felt that "this was the nicest of the camps," so they bought it. "It was rustic and required a lot of physical work, as well as being financially challenging," recalled Marilyn, "but we were young and didn't know any better."

The camp (in 1996) offered a balanced program of sports, including horseback riding, tennis, swimming, water-skiing, sailing and other boating experiences, dance/drama, archery and special events. Marilyn described the atmosphere as

Campers at the one-hundred-acre Camp Kiniya in the Clay Point area of town, founded circa 1920, for girls seven to seventeen years of age. *Courtesy of Marilyn and Jack Williams.*

> *old-fashioned fun within a wholesome community. Our campers cannot bring radios, walkmans are allowed only at night and there's no television. They learn to be self-sufficient—we've never heard a camper say they are bored. We also offer a cultural experience here unlike that found in many other camps because of the diversity of campers and counselors. We have campers from Hong Kong, Iran, etc., and counselors are from Britain and Australia, among other places.*

Campers today are girls, ages seven to seventeen years old. The cost is $601 to $700 per week, and the camp is ACA approved. Summing up the program, Marilyn said, "We're a community that sets values that are good for the kids and encourages them to care about each other."

In 1996, when an interview was conducted with Father Richard LaValley of Camp Holy Cross, it was about to celebrate its fiftieth anniversary. The camp, however, closed at the end of the 2008 season, sixty-two years after it opened its doors to sixty campers, six to fifteen years of age, per session. For all of those years, it never changed its focus of offering a sound Christian adventure and fun-filled experience for boys. It later offered a coed day camp. A comparable camp for girls using the same facilities was run by the Junior Catholic Daughters and was held the second week of August. As a

Catholic-run facility, campers would celebrate daily Mass and an evening prayer time for reflection, as well as enjoying water-related sports, arts and crafts and other special events.

The camp was originally owned by the Barnard School Corporation and was called Camp Barnard. An additional three and a half acres were bought from Albert and Louise Bosley and added to the existing fifteen acres. Right Reverend Edward J. Fitzsimons was the first camp director, serving for twelve years. Other directors included Father Basil Nichols of Rutland and Staneslaws Receyek, according to *Look Around Colchester and Milton, Vermont*, by the Chittenden Historical Society.

Another camp run by the Catholic Diocese and located next door to Camp Holy Cross was Camp Tara. Here, roughly forty weekly campers, boys and girls ages seven to twelve years, who normally would be unable to afford a summer camp experience, gathered for a week at a time to enjoy the lake and several other new and exciting ventures. The philosophy of the camp was to give children the opportunity to make friends, expand their outlook and work toward a more satisfying life, according to then director Jim Osbourne.

Founded in 1958 as Camp Tara, it had formerly been a commercial camp called Camp Iroquois, according to the Chittenden Historical Society book. Henry and Mary Carse bought it, named it Tara after a county in Ireland and then donated it to the Catholic Diocese, saying that they wanted to have a place for Vermont kids who could not afford such an experience. It, too, consisted of fifteen acres with five hundred feet of lakeshore. Sadly, this camp closed in 2007.

Lasting just one week a summer, Camp Ta Kum Ta leased facilities from Camp Holy Cross for twenty-four years. Serving Vermont's most special children—those who have or have had cancer—the camp ended that relationship in 2008, when the Catholic Diocese announced that it would be selling Camp Holy Cross. However, Camp Ta Kum Ta secured its own home in the Champlain Islands and was able to continue into its twenty-fifth year serving children from seven to seventeen years of age. With an all-volunteer staff of up to seventy people (one on one with the campers), the camp offers water sports, arts and crafts, lots of fun games, boat rides, hot-air balloon rides, dances, area tours, special appearances from surprise guests (such as the Vermont Expos and Larry, Daryl and Daryl of the old Bob Newhart Show) and especially the opportunity to interact with one another.

"Everyone is so nice…they help us to believe that we may have some problems being sick, but we are OK…we're normal," said one camper. The name is said to have come from then four-year-old Natasha Sainz, who one day, at the clinic for her treatment, said, "I wanta cometa camp." The phrase stuck, and so did she (she came to camp for many years after). For more information, call Camp Director Ted Kessler at (802) 244-5333 or e-mail takumta@aol.com.

As of 2009, Colchester is still host to two commercial camps and its own public day camps at the Bayside Park on Malletts Bay offered through the Recreation Department. For more information on these coed day programs, call (802) 264-5640.

IRA ALLEN

The Link Between Communities

Not only is Ira Allen credited as being one of the founders of the state of Vermont and the founder of the University of Vermont, but he is also the key to any discussion of the history of Colchester and Winooski. This is a look at the man, his relevance to both communities and some of his exploits.

A "flatlander," Allen was born in Cornwall, Connecticut, on May 1, 1751, to Joseph Allen and Mary Baker, who were farmers. As an adult, he is described in Ruth Wright's book *Colchester, Vermont: Ice-Cap to Interstate*, as having brown hair and large brown eyes set in a handsome face. He was well built, but not as tall as his brothers. In his autobiography, *Ira Allen, Founder of Vermont, 1751–1814*, he adds that his nickname was "Stub."

At nineteen years of age, he followed his five elder brothers north to the New Hampshire Grants region and joined the "Yankee" versus "Yorker" struggle. A 1764 Crown degree stated that New York, rather than New Hampshire, was entitled to the area then known as New Connecticut, later to be called Vermont. Allen first purchased land in Poultney and Hubbardton, and while working to clear the land, he got wind of Yorkers surveying the Onion River area. In the summer of 1772, Ira learned that this surveyor "was gone to the Onion River." He persuaded his brother, Heman, to give him a two-hundred-pound letter of credit and entered into a partnership with his cousin, Remember Baker, to hire help and furnish provisions to go north. "I contemplated the extent of the New Hampshire Grants and probable advantages that might arise by being contiguous to Lake Champlain," he wrote.

With five other men, they set out from Crown Point by boat. The little boat became wind bound in "Shelburn," but Ira, minus two men who decided to go on through the woods, continued on to the Onion River Falls. He found what he suspected to be the surveyor's camp. Ira and his men lay in wait for the return of the surveying party, and when they arrived, Ira—his company now enlarged by the addition of ten Indians and four more of his surveying crew—confronted them with a show of weapons. He wrote, "When about 30 feet of me, I presented a pistol at him, with a solemn word that death was his portion instantly if he stepped one step further." Thinking better of killing the Yorkers, he wrote,

> *We thought it would not be politic to inflict corporal punishment on Stevens—he and his men were dismissed on pain of death never to come within the district of the New Hampshire Grants again. Their boats and store were also returned to them and we parted.*

Allen took the occasion of this incident to survey the area and was enamored with the intervals below the falls of the Onion River.

> *I went up the open meadow where the blue joint grass was thick till in sight of a large and lonely elm…I was much pleased with this excursion promising myself one day to be the owner of that beautiful meadow.*

Because of his enthusiasm for the land, he persuaded his brothers, Ethan, Heman, Heber and Zimri, along with Remember Baker, to form the Onion River Land Company in 1773. "My brothers began to listen to my proposition to purchase lands and extend settlement to Onion River," he wrote. The plan of the company was to purchase lands and furnish stores to commence settlement in the towns of Burlington, Williston, Shelburn, Colchester, Essex and Jericho. Because New York and New Hampshire were still warring, Ethan attended to the political affairs (leading the Green Mountain Boys), while Baker and Ira took care of business on the Onion River. According to volume one of the *American National Biography*, by the start of the American Revolution, the company's partners had amassed holdings of sixty-five thousand acres as the first step in Ira's plan for achieving personal and family wealth.

Ira had selected a knoll overlooking the valley as the site for his house. He set apple trees on the slopes, which ran down to the river between its upper and lower falls (*Ice-Cap*). The spot described is where the Winooski Block now stands. The widow of Ira's brother Heber kept Ira's home. Her son, Heman, was adopted by Ira. In 1789 (the year his brother Ethan died), Ira married twenty-five-year-old Jerusha Enos and gave her the town of Irasburg as a wedding present. They had three children—Ira Hayden, born in 1790; Zimri, born in 1792; and Marie Juliet, born in 1794. Juliet died at seventeen years of age and Zimri at twenty-one, just as he was preparing to practice law.

Colchester's first town meeting was held on March 23, 1774, with Colonel Thomas Chittenden serving as moderator. Ira Allen was voted to be the "clark" of the town and its official surveyor, according to *Colchester First Book of Records*. At that same meeting, the Allens (and Remember Baker), who composed the Onion River Company, were given "Liberty to Pitch and Lay out with what they have laid out on Sd river fifteen Hundred acres in Hundred acres Lots."

With his faith in the future of the area, Ira, in 1791, with £4,000 of his own money, started a college for the Champlain Valley and later convinced the state legislature to select Burlington to be the home of the newly chartered University of Vermont. In explaining his reasons for founding the university, he wrote:

> *It is not the rich that I am calculating so much to assist as the poor. The rich can send their sons to what college they choose, but the poor have it not in their power yet they may have the most promising posterity and if they can obtain good educations may be in turn rulers of the land.*

Since Lake Champlain connected Vermont to Canada, according to the *American National Biography*, Ira

> *hinted to the British that independent Vermont might still rejoin the empire and collaborated with his brother Levi to ship Vermont lumber and agricultural products north in exchange for cash and European manufactured goods.*

The venture was not successful, however, and in the mid-1790s, the brothers found themselves in debt in Quebec and elsewhere. Desperate in 1795, Allen mortgaged forty-five thousand acres of his best lands and sailed to England, where he hoped to get permission to build a ship canal

A statute of Ira Allen on the campus of the University of Vermont. *Photo by Hank Schaefer.*

from St. John to the St. Lawrence River north of Montreal to improve transatlantic trade. Unsuccessful in England, he traveled to France, asking that country to back a democratic revolution in British Canada. France agreed, and in November 1796, with fifteen thousand muskets to equip French-Canadian and American recruits, Ira left on the American ship the

Olive Branch. Unfortunately, the British, who accused Ira of buying the guns for the French resistance, intercepted the ship. He spent the next five years in litigation actions, including almost one year of imprisonment in France as a British spy.

When he returned to Vermont in 1801, he found his fortune gone. In her book, Wright notes:

> *Creditors and enemies, including members of his own family (land records show Lucinda Allen Catlin, only daughter of his brother Heman, and her husband Moses Catlin on Nov. 13, 1798 "attached the whole township of Colchester" and secured judgment of $46,728.96 and costs of $118.84) snatched at the opportunity to take great portions of Ira's holdings. To avoid debtor's prison, he fled (in the middle of the night) south to Philadelphia where he spent the last decade of his life, estranged from his family, publishing pamphlets and trying to recover his losses.*

In 1811, the following advertisement was seen in local northern Vermont newspapers:

> *FOR SALE: A valuable farm in Colchester, on the bank of the Onion River at the Lower Falls adjoining Burlington about one mile and a half from the College. On the premise there is a handsome convenient dwelling, house, barns…a good garden well stored with fruit and two bearing apple orchards. The situation of the house is healthy and agreeable, affording delightful views.*

Upon the sale of the Allen homestead, Mrs. Allen and her son, Ira H. Allen, left to live in Irasburg. Ira Allen died a pauper on January 14, 1814, and his body went to an unmarked grave in the city's Free Quaker Cemetery (see related article).

Ira Allen served as Vermont's state treasurer from 1778 to 1786 and as the town's legislative representative in 1785 and again in 1794.

Allen was a prolific and articulate writer, as the following excerpts from the appendix of Ira Allen's *History of the State of Vermont*, published in 1798 in London, England, demonstrate. On the subject of the inhabitants of the state, Allen wrote:

> *I am really at a loss in the classification of the inhabitants—they are all farmers, and again every farmer is a mechanic in some line or*

other, as inclination leads or necessity requires. The hand that leads the plough frequently constructs it, and the labours of the axe and the plane often evince a degree of genius and dexterity that would really amaze you…When a new settler arrives, it is not material from what part of the world he came, industry and a good character are the best recommendations, and if he brings these with him, he is received with hospitality and kindness.

Regarding the succession of seasons, he wrote:

Spring pays its welcome visit in April, and is soon followed by summer, October and November are pleasant and the rest of the year is resigned to the rigid reign of winter…The weather, however is sometimes capricious, a fall of snow serves as a covering to inhale the radical moisture of the earth, and as it is replete with nitre, it supplies the place of manure, and when it is gradually dissolved, vegetation shoots forth in the highest luxuriancy.

Concerning the fair sex, he mused:

I scarce know of any nation that pays a greater deference to the fair sex than the Americans, and very deservedly too, for it is but justice to my fair country-woman to say that they are highly worthy of it in every situation, maid, wife and widow…Our Vermontese house-wives are not a little vain of their knowledge in making home-made wines, such as gooseberry, raspberry, etc., these native productions are exceedingly pleasing, refreshing and healthy.

And finally, Allen wrote:

If you favour this country with a visit, you will find that I have only failed in one thing, and that is, that my descriptive powers cannot do justice to the fertility and beauty of the country, to the hospitality of its inhabitants, to the plenty that is found in every house and the content that is pictured in every countenance, and that reigns in every heart—would that all mankind were as happy this minute as the Vermontese.

Winooski—The Wayward Kin

Though just a small area of Colchester, Winooski played a major role in the growth of the town—much of it due to its relationship to the river. Archaeologists from the University of Vermont have conducted studies in the area, and their analysis shows, according to *The Great Falls on Onion River: A History of Winooski, Vermont* by Vincent Edward Feeney, "that it [the Winooski area] had been intermittently occupied from 3000 BC to about 1000 AD." The Abenakis spoke of a village named Winooskik on the lower reaches of a river referred to by the tribe as the "Onion River" or "Winooski." At ninety miles, the Winooski is the longest river within the boundaries of the state of Vermont. The name "Winooski" is composed of two Indian words: *winos* meaning "onions," and *ki*, the word for "land." According to the *Burlington Free Press* quoting the *Geography and History of Vermont* (1965), it was also called the Onion River, having the same meaning as Winooski for the abundance of wild onions that grew on its banks.

When Ira Allen arrived in 1772, he found a camp that belonged to a (New) "Yorker" surveyor. He and his men "persuaded" the surveyor and his party to abandon the camp and to return from whence they had come. Quick to recognize the potential of the land surrounding "the Fall," Allen formed the Onion River Company, along with his brothers, Ethan, Heber, Heman and Zimbry, and cousin, Remember Baker. The company began farming, built a dam and gristmills and offered other amenities to settlers, such as Fort Frederick, built in 1773 to provide protection and a location for social gatherings. The area quickly became an industrial and commercial hub.

According to Feeney, this section was referred to as either "Colchester Falls," "Burlington Falls" or simply "the Falls." He noted that when the Indian name came back into fashion after the threat of Indian attacks had passed, the name "Winooski Falls," and later just Winooski, was generally adopted. "By 1791, the first U.S. Census reported that Colchester had 137 residents—most of them would have been located near the Falls," Feeney writes.

In the years to follow the development sparked by Ira Allen, others came and built an oil mill and a five-story gristmill (constructed by Moses Catlin). Not too long after, in 1838, the first textile mill was built. Stores and shops appeared, along with assorted boardinghouses, taverns, small houses and even, Feeney notes, "a hotel built in 1830 by Arad Merrill." By the 1850s, Feeney continues, "due to hard times in Quebec—there had been a steady

Looking east on Main Street, Winooski, circa 1870. *Courtesy of Arthur Daley.*

stream of French Canadians to the Falls, all looking for work. The same was true of Irish emigrants." While this diverse population, including others from Italy, Germany, England and Scotland, was settling in the small area called Winooski, the rural part of Colchester remained inhabited primarily by "Yankees."

In 1850, the population of Colchester was 2,575, but it had steadily increased to 3,911 by 1870, particularly in the new village of Winooski, according to Ruth Wright. Colchester's rural farmers made trips to "the Falls" to sell eggs, butter, apples, vegetables and other farm produce. During the War of 1812, the woolen industry so mushroomed that Colchester farmers had to increase their sheep herds in order to meet the demand and still have enough to take care of their own needs. According to Wright's book, a farmer might on occasion indulge at a local watering hole, where, in order to close for the night, the bar owner would "set and prop the inebriated torso in its wagon, wrap the reins around the whip socket and slap the horse on the flank. Over the miles of sand-rutted roads, the soused rider was safely toted."

Politically, the settling immigrants found comfort in the Democratic party, while the farmers in rural Colchester chose the philosophy of the Republicans.

A view looking west on Main Street, circa 1870s. *Courtesy of Arthur Daley.*

St. Francis Xavier Church, built in 1868. *Courtesy of the Winooski Historical Society.*

While the town residents generally adhered to Protestant religions and attended the Baptist, Congregational or Methodist churches located in the village area, the immigrant French-Canadians, usually Catholic, had to wait until the late 1860s to be able to worship in their first neighborhood Catholic church, St. Francis Xavier, in 1868.

Even the schools demonstrated the societal differences between urban Winooski Falls and rural Colchester. One need only look at the school report of 1864. School District No. 6 represented the Winooski area and listed 602 students, with a grand list expenditure of $941.73. The rest of the town had thirteen school districts, with as few as 11 students in one district or school and no more than 67 in another, with average attendance at about 36 students per school. Clearly, the population was more concentrated in Winooski, while in rural Colchester, families were spread out, drawing together for church or other social or civic gatherings.

Because of the need for uniforms, etc., the Civil War in the 1860s proved to be a boon for the Winooski mills, which expanded their facilities and installed new equipment. "A recession in the 1870s slowed economic growth and produced wholesale unemployment," *Look Around Winooski, Vermont*, by the Chittenden County Historical Society notes. The Burlington Woolen Company was forced into bankruptcy in the late 1890s, but the American Woolen Company took it over and even expanded by building the Champlain Mill east of the bridge in 1912. With the onset of the national recession following the end of World War I, the American Woolen Company laid off its workers in Winooski and closed its doors by 1921. Feeney writes that talks of joining Winooski to Burlington or becoming a city went back as far as the mid-1880s, but following the closing of the American Woolen Mill and the subsequent economic crisis in the village, "citizens argued that supporting two local governments was inefficient, and that rural Colchester was uninterested in funding Winooski's urban needs."

By 1900, the town of Colchester, including Winooski, had grown to 5,352 people. Its twenty-one thousand acres of land and buildings were appraised at $1,116,992. In 1914, East Allen Street was chosen as the location for the town clerk's office, which would contain a vault that would house the town and village records. The records that existed for the town and the village through 1922 would remain in Winooski until 2008, when Colchester opened its new town hall with sufficient vault capacity to accommodate the earlier records. On June 9, 1921, the voters of the village of Winooski were asked to meet in the hall on Main Street at ten

A mill on the Winooski River. *Courtesy of Rebecca Munson and the Colchester Historical Society.*

o'clock in the forenoon to transact the following business: "To see if the Village will vote to adopt the Charter for the proposed city of Winooski enacted by the General Assembly of the State of Vermont of 1921." According to the Winooski Historical Society, the vote of only Winooski Village residents was 176 for, with 78 against.

The city's first mayor, H. Albon Bailey, said of the split:

> *For more than twenty years* [following the village incorporation in 1867] *there had been more or less agitation for incorporating the village of Winooski as a city. It has been recognized that the interests of industrial Winooski and rural Colchester are so different that it would be of mutual advantage to separate.*

In a *Burlington Free Press* article, C.A.G. Jackson commented:

> *Long overshadowed by its proximity to its larger neighbor, Burlington, Winooski expects to receive a larger share of attention and to become better known when the new form of government* [city] *places the municipality in the higher and "classier" rank.*

The *Burlington Free Press*, in an editorial on March 6, 1922, reported the split: "Tomorrow will see the dawn of a new era for Winooski…this day is looked on by some as a great mistake and by others as the beginning of a new and brighter day for Winooski." Following the 1922 separation, Winooski was left with one square mile of land, or 795 acres.

OFT FORGOTTEN...SO MUCH TO SAY, SO LITTLE SPACE

What is history but a fable agreed upon?
—Napoleon Bonaparte

Approximately 246 years of history is not easily condensed into 144 pages. These few remaining items offer further depth to a community rich in diversity. In my previous book, *Images of America: Colchester*, I wrote:

> *From its sandy soils in Malletts Bay to its fine clays found in the Clay Point area to its wetlands and rocky hills, Colchester holds as much contrast in its topography and geology as it does in its assortment of waterways.*

The Winooski and Lamoille Rivers border the town on the north and south, with the breathtaking Colchester Pond also to the north. Malletts Bay, the largest bay on Lake Champlain, lies to the southwest, along with miles of shoreline on the broad lake between Vermont and New York.

Farmers, millers and tradesmen constituted the occupations of the early rural settlers in Colchester, while the hustle and bustle of the Winooski Falls area offered jobs as factory and mill workers to French-Canadian and other immigrants. This difference, among others, eventually led to a split with Winooski, which became a city in 1922. In 2009, Colchester is still rooted in its agrarian heritage, despite having only three remaining dairy farms. Today, several horse stables can be found, along with nurseries, vegetable farms, an egg farm and honeybee and maple sugaring operations. Most residents work for such nearby companies as IBM, the University of Vermont, Fletcher Allen Health Care Center or one of several companies located in the Exit 16 (off Interstate 89) area of town.

As a result of the commercial and financial activity centered at the Falls, the town of Colchester lost its opportunity to firmly establish a town center. From the beginning, there have been four distinct areas of town—the village, Clay Point, Malletts Bay and Fort Ethan Allen; however, in recent years, progress toward establishing a "downtown" or town center has begun. With three schools; a new town office (opened in 2008); police, rescue and highway department buildings; and a post office nearby, the area of Blakely Road (at the intersection with Malletts Bay Avenue) is shaping up to be the new center of civic activity for Colchester. A community center is being considered for this area, as well, and may include a library satellite, a senior citizen component, recreational facilities for young and old and meeting rooms.

Before concluding this look at Colchester history, there are some historic tidbits that amplify the diversity of this community that the reader may find interesting. For instance, at Camp Johnson, just as you enter the Army National Guard base, on the right rests Vermont's only military museum. Called the Vermont Veterans Militia Museum and Library (VVMML), it holds memorabilia from the Revolutionary War to the Iraq War, with military uniforms, weaponry and documents dating back to 1790. The centerpiece of the museum is one of the largest oil paintings in the world, entitled *Sheridan's Ride*. The VVMML brochure notes that "the 17' x 28' panorama was painted after the Civil War to honor the great sacrifices of Vermonters who served in that struggle." Outside the museum are several pieces of army equipment too large to be exhibited indoors, such as a tank, a jet fighter, artillery pieces and a helicopter.

Every exhibit has an interesting story, but one that catches the eye is the display on Sergeant Florence (Weidinger) MacAlister, who was one of the first six female marines to be sworn into service in 1918. She was later buried across the street from Camp Johnson at the military cemetery. Among the outside attractions is a four-barrel antiaircraft weapon, 14.5 mm, of Czech design that was "borrowed" from Saddam Hussein's army during the Gulf War. When the Vermont Guard unit went to the Gulf, it was told to bring back souvenirs, and this was one. The free (no admission charge) museum has been expanded in recent years and is open every Tuesday from 10:00 a.m. to 3:00 p.m. For more information, call (802) 338-3360.

A Civil War uniform on display at the Vermont Veterans Militia Museum and Library. *Photo by Inge Schaefer.*

Niquette State Park, in the Clay Point area of town, is home to at least one prehistoric site. "It dates from the late Archaic period (6,000–3,000 years ago)," according to a management plan for the park prepared by University of Vermont student Hilary Batson. The plan concludes that there is a good likelihood that other archaeological sites are located in the park. The park was originally purchased by the state

> *in response to the expressed need of the Vermont State Parks Division for additional facilities on the water, to accommodate recreational demand in a populous region and to relieve congestion at the Sand Bar State Park, located up the road a piece.*

This property, after Europeans settled the area, was farmed and logged intensively. The ruins of the Allen farmstead are still visible today in the eastern section of the parcel. The farmstead was thought to have been established sometime between 1857 and 1871 and finally abandoned in the 1940s. According to the *Colchester News Magazine* of May 1996, "At the northern end of the park, evidence has been found of jasper quarrying activity from the historic period."

State lands' forester David Brynn, in the management report, lists the following timber growing in the park: sugar maple, hickory, beech, butternut, red oak, white cedar, white pine, aspen, hemlock, white ash, white birch and saw timber. A stand of *Quercus muhlenbergii*, quite rare in Vermont, has also been identified. According to Brynn, "Wildlife species on the property include white-tailed deer, cottontail rabbit, snowshoe hare, gray squirrel, ruffed grouse, wild turkey, beaver, muskrat, red fox, raccoon and skunk." He adds that there is occasional use by waterfowl, mink, otters, bobcats, coyotes and fishers, with year-round residents including porcupines and woodchucks. There are a wide variety of forest bird species, plus the great horned owl, barred owl and red-tailed hawk that stop by. In 1986, UVM Department of Zoology professors discovered a rare species of slavemaker ant called *Leptothorax duloticus Wesson* at the park. According to Robin J. Stuart, one of the two professors involved in the discovery:

> *This is the only record of* L. duloticus *in Vermont and only one of a handful overall. It quickly stings and kills defending host workers during slave raids and recruits nest mates during raids in processions that can include up to forty ants following a leader from the slavemaker nest to the host nest.*

Sailing and boating on Malletts Bay have long been popular, and one of the most active groups to provide access for sailors to the lake was the Malletts Bay Boat Club (MBBC), founded in 1936. After ice severely damaged the piers of the Lake Champlain Yacht Club (LCYC) on the Burlington waterfront, some of the members came north to Colchester while the rest went south to Shelburne Bay. There is also the rumor that the seven founding members of the MBBC were tired of the "high falutin social atmosphere" of the LCYC. This could explain why they called it a "boat club" instead of a "yacht club."

They first built a clubhouse on leased land west of the present location on Lakeshore Drive. The first winter was spent constructing a small fleet of snipe-class sailboats that were registered with the national association.

Boating chores remain the same today as those faced by this young lady of earlier days. *Courtesy of the David Coates family and Greg Dirmaier.*

An old steam-powered motorboat in Malletts Bay. *Courtesy of the David Coates family and Greg Dirmaier.*

The club's first race week was held in August 1937. In January 1938, the first piece of MBBC property was purchased on Lakeshore Drive. In the early 1950s, an adjoining camp and property were purchased, and again in 1985, more property was acquired to allow the club to expand its mooring capabilities.

The club temporarily suspended operation until World War II ended, and shortly thereafter, in 1947, the club was officially incorporated. In those early days, powerboats outnumbered sailboats. For instance, in 1959, there were 40 powerboats and 34 sailboats. In 1996, there were 157 sailboats and 4 powerboats, and in this past 2008 season, there were 137 sailboats and 19 powerboats. In 1954, Bill and Dawn Hazelett started sailing classes with boats borrowed in the summer months from UVM and St. Michael's College. They later negotiated with a boat manufacturer in Holland to buy sailboat kits to make thirty Indian Scouts, the official boat of the Royal Dutch Yachting Society. The Junior Sailing Program has flourished ever since. A new boathouse was built and opened in 1980. (Information on the MBBC was found in Ken Wolvington's history of the MBBC and from Jonathan Haas, harbormaster of the club.)

Joel Farnsworth, in the early 1900s, was known as the telephone pioneer of New England. *Courtesy of the Colchester Historical Society.*

Colchester had its own Alexander Graham Bell in Joel Farnsworth, who said of himself:

> *I have been called the telephone pioneer of New England. Having been in the telephone business longer than any other man I might say that when I sold my lines I owned the largest telephone plant in New England owned and operated entirely by one person. I had no partners or stockholders.*

Farnsworth was born in Cambridge, Vermont, in 1858 and moved to Colchester in 1859. His schooling was primarily in District No. 2, but he lost one year of school at the age of ten when he was in bed for fourteen weeks with typhoid fever. He was on crutches for a year following his illness. After thirteen years of age, he only attended school in the winter months, as it was the custom for children of that age to work during the summer.

Farnsworth recalled:

> *I started the Central Telephone Company in business in 1890. I began wiring Colchester with telegraph wires in 1875 and later converted them to*

telephone lines. About this time I was held up by the Bell Company because of patent rights and had to go back to the telegraph for a few years. I made my own telephones and built lines and sold the phones to patrons of my lines. I found that this method was rather slow, as I could not get enough people to build lines and own their phones. So, in 1900, I began to build lines and rent phones at $10 a year. I found it hard work to build lines and phones as fast as I got orders for them. I soon found that I had 350 miles of wire and 300 subscribers. In 1920 I sold my lines to C.L. Ovitt, who later sold to the Central Company. For 12 years I worked for this company taking care of my plant for them. But after the lines were sold to the New England Telephone and Telegraph Company, I only worked two months as they let me out on account of my age.

Joel Wilson Farnsworth died on February 16, 1942, at the age of eighty-three years. (Much of this information was originally from the 1939 Burlington Suburban List and was reprinted in *Colchester Past*, a publication of the Colchester Historical Society.)

While postal service began in Vermont in 1794 in Newbury and four other southern towns, it took until 1813 for the first post office to open in Colchester Center. Ruth Wright writes in her book, "The basement of the dwelling, at the brow of the hill, whose big, stout door opened directly on the east side of the East Road, was the early post office." News was also carried by a stage that ran through Colchester from Rutland to Highgate and a British carrier that traveled through Colchester between Montreal and Burlington every fortnight. The village post office served the entire town until January 1881.

After a petition for a post office was approved, the post office of Mallett (notice the absence of the *s*) Bay was established, with Alexander C. Morrison appointed in 1882 as postmaster (he was actually the second appointed postmaster after Charles L. Sanford, who refused the position). Unfortunately, Morrison was paid on the basis of the postage sold, but he soon discovered that he was selling too few postage stamps and spending too much time sorting newspapers and periodicals. He resigned in 1884 and turned the job over to Willard Thayer, who was willing to perform the work in order to lure more customers to his store. He, too, soon found that the amount of mail did not warrant his taking the trouble to change the date in his postmarking hand stamp every day. That being the case, he did not bother to change it every month or even every year. He simply struck each envelope with the hand stamp twice, once for the postmark and again to

Rural Free Delivery (RFD) in earlier times. Colchester still offers some RFD postal services, but in 2009, it no longer carries stamps for sale. *Courtesy of Greg Dirmaier.*

cancel the stamp. He then filled in the date with pen and ink. In 1901, the Mallett Bay Post Office was discontinued. In 2009, Colchester has one post office on Malletts Bay Avenue serving the entire community.

The oldest identified site in Colchester might be the Colchester Bog off Colchester Point Road in Malletts Bay. It dates back nine thousand years. As the Neolithic Revolution of 7000 BC was taking place, the Colchester Bog was beginning to form in an old channel of the Winooski River. When humans were just starting to domesticate sheep, goats and cattle, perfecting their speech, learning to weave baskets and designing weapons and jewelry from copper, bronze and gold, the bog was becoming a peat land. Not only does the age of the Colchester Bog single it out as a unique natural area, but it is also the only bog in the state to be located alongside the shores of a lake. University of Vermont's Ian Worley (UVM is the steward for the bog, which is considered a national landmark), says:

> *It is a natural library recording the history of the lake and the mouth of the Winooski since the last day the ice left—10,000 to 12,000 years ago. Because of its relationship to the shoreline, it floods every spring, allowing the lake to provide nutrients to the bog rather than have them come for other sources. It is the only bog to flood like that.*

The Vermont Chapter of the Nature Conservancy originally purchased the bog in 1973 from a 175-acre tract from Donald O'Brien and a 25-acre piece from Paul Porter on the condition that it maintain, protect and manage

The Colchester Bog walkway, 1996. *Photo by Inge Schaefer.*

it as a natural area. It was turned over to UVM in 1974 for research and educational purposes.

The process of bog formation is triggered when a body of essentially static water becomes oxygen poor, reducing the decaying of organic matter falling into it. Gradually, this accumulated organic matter, called peat, builds up and provides the substrate for a mat of sphagnum moss and sedges. The bog's peat averages three meters in depth, with some areas exceeding six meters. Deep in the bog, such plants as orchids (rose pagonia, grass pink and arethusa varieties), bog rosemary, bog laurel, tawny cotton grass and small and large cranberries can be found. The bog is also home to insect-eating plants, including round-leaved sundew, pitcher plant and bladderwort. Maples, white cedars and small groves of white and pitch pine, along with holly, rhodora and barador-tea scrubs, can be found.

A short boardwalk just off Airport Park was constructed in 1996 to protect the trampling of plants and the "open mat" (the spongy low areas of the bog). That structure is in the process of being replaced, according to Rick Paradis, director of Natural Areas Center at the University of Vermont: "The old hemlock planking will be replaced with European Larch planking taken from trees on another university property, which should last far longer than the original boardwalk."

With its many treasures and its broad diversity, the quiet, rural hamlet that began in 1763 remains. Colchester, the sleeping giant, appears to still be at rest.